Community Building: What Makes It Work

Community Building: What Makes It Work

A Review of Factors Influencing Successful Community Building

By   Paul Mattessich, Ph.D.
      Barbara Monsey, M.P.H.
      with assistance from Corinna Roy, M.A.

      Wilder Research Center

Amherst H. Wilder Foundation
Saint Paul, Minnesota

This book was developed by Wilder Research Center, a program of the Amherst H. Wilder Foundation in Saint Paul, Minnesota. Wilder Research Center provides community studies, social trend/demographic studies, demonstration studies, consultation research, research studies, and a newsletter, *findings*.

The Amherst H. Wilder Foundation is one of the largest and oldest endowed human service and community development organizations in America. For more than ninety years, the Wilder Foundation has been providing health and human services that help children and families grow strong, the elderly age with dignity, and the community grow in its ability to meet its own needs.

We hope you find this report helpful! Should you need additional information about our research services, please contact: Wilder Research Center, Amherst H. Wilder Foundation, 1295 Bandana Boulevard North, Suite 210, Saint Paul, MN 55108, (612) 647-4600.

For information about other Wilder Foundation publications, please see the order form on the last page or contact: Publishing Center, Amherst H. Wilder Foundation, 919 Lafond Avenue, Saint Paul, MN 55104, 1-800-274-6024.

Edited by Vincent Hyman
Cover Illustration by Fran Gregory
Designed by Rebecca Andrews

Manufactured in the United States of America

First printing, April 1997

Library of Congress Cataloging-in-Publication Data

Mattessich, Paul W.
     Community building : what makes it work : a review of factors influencing successful community building / by Paul Mattessich, Barbara Monsey, with assistance from Corinna Roy.
          p.   cm.
     Includes bibliographical references.
     ISBN 0-940069-12-1 (paperback)
     1. Community development--Research.   2. Community organization--Research.   3. Community power--Research.   I. Monsey, Barbara R.   II. Roy, Corinna.   III. Title.
HN49.C6M3293 1997   97-12500
307.1'4'072--dc21   CIP

Acknowledgments

The authors wish to thank the many people we talked with and gathered advice from about this project. In particular, we are grateful for the advice and comments from those who reviewed drafts of this report: Peter Benson, Kim Bobo, Arthur Bolton, John Couchman, Amy Crawford, Tracy Curts, Barbara Davis, Nancy Devitt, Audrey Faulkner, Linda Garrett-Johnson, Robert Giloth, Richard Goebel, Ruth Goins, Carole Hamner, Anne Kubisch, Nancy Latimer, Carol Lukas, Jan Morlock, Andy Mott, Carol Ogren, Pat Peterson, Judy Sharken Simon, Harold Simon, Rebecca Stone, Abby Struck, Mercer Sullivan, and Patti Tototzintle.

Our colleagues at Wilder Research Center, Phil Cooper and Marilyn Conrad, provided helpful assistance with word processing and database development. Other colleagues at the Research Center provided helpful advice and support. Bryan Barry and Vince Hyman of the Wilder Foundation provided the initial impetus for this project. We would like to thank them for their involvement, support, and patience. We are grateful for the support of our funders:

Ewing Marion Kauffman Foundation

Indianapolis Neighborhood Center

Local Initiatives Support Corporation

McKnight Foundation

The Saint Paul Foundation

3M Foundation

About the Authors

Paul W. Mattessich, Ph.D., is director of Wilder Research Center, which conducts research related to human services trends, programs, and policies. Mattessich has been involved in applied social research since 1973. He lectures and consults with nonprofit organizations, foundations, and government throughout the United States and is the author or co-author of more than one hundred publications and reports. He has also served on a variety of task forces in government and the nonprofit sectors. He received his Ph.D. in Sociology from the University of Minnesota.

Barbara R. Monsey, M.P.H., is a research associate at Wilder Research Center and managing editor of the newsletter, *findings*. She has co-authored two other literature review reports for practitioners: *Collaboration, What Makes it Work* and *What Works in Preventing Rural Violence: Strategies, Risk Factors, and Assessment Tools*. She has a master's degree in Public Health Education from the University of North Carolina.

Contents

Chapter One
Introduction

*O*n West 119th street in Harlem . . .

residents are noticing changes in the neighborhood. "It's beginning to grow again. It's getting clean again. There are young minds bringing us together," says long-time resident, 86-year-old Marguerite Gordon. The young and the old are coming together to build new relationships with one another, advocate for repairs in housing, and seek better services. What they're gaining is a stronger sense of mutual responsibility.

On West 119th street, housing conditions are bad and drugs and violence are ever present. But the community also has a well-established church, a cooperative apartment building that tenants purchased from the city, and a number of long-time residents with experience and commitment to the community. Community Pride, a neighborhood organizing project, is building on these strengths by organizing community celebrations and block parties, offering tutoring sessions for students, and holding small weekly worship sessions during the summer and holidays.

This block in Harlem is being considered in the City's initiative to rehabilitate and sell city-owned buildings to small businesses, neighborhood nonprofits, and tenants themselves. Community residents hope to be educated and organized enough to take action when neighborhood housing owned by the city is sold in the near future.[1]

---

[1] This case was summarized from an article in *City Limits*, New York's Urban Affairs News Magazine.

In the small, rural community of Ivanhoe, Virginia ...

the closing of major industries created an economic crisis and leadership vacuum. Local residents found it hard to fill the leadership vacuum and to advocate for their community. Many believed there was nothing they could do to help themselves.

Out of such hopelessness came amazing changes. A group of community members started attending seminars to gain skills in community organizing and leadership building. Fledgling community leaders learned how to lead meetings, how to use the media, how to communicate effectively, and how to raise money. They began to understand how political and economic systems work—and how to influence those systems to benefit the community. They developed a sense of pride. They gained confidence in their own ability to understand and act on that understanding. They organized community members, held discussion groups, and planned community meetings and events. These activities led to increased support, momentum, organizing skills, leadership skills, and ultimately, a sense of hope that the community could put itself back on track. A crusade to recruit industry and revitalize the community was in full swing.[2]

In Oakland, California ...

a group of low-income residents and new immigrants organized to address unmet health care needs. Working door-to-door and through key community leaders, they recruited community residents. The community members met over potluck dinners and in discussion groups. As they became comfortable with one another, they started to make suggestions for addressing their most important need: immunizations for their children.[3]

In northern Sierra Leone, Africa ...

villagers routinely spent hours searching for water, sometimes traveling up to six kilometers. Fifteen village women organized to find support for an improved village well. They selected two women to represent them in a meeting with the village chief. A village meeting was held and the villagers

[2] This case was summarized from the book *It Comes from the People: Community Development and Local Theology* by Mary Ann Hinsdale, Helen M. Lewis, and S. Maxine Waller.

[3] This case was summarized from the chapter "Building Multiracial Alliances: the Case of People United for a Better Oakland" by Gary Delgado in the book *Mobilizing the Community: Local Politics in the Era of the Global City.*

agreed to form a committee of five, to include the assistant chief, the head of the young adult males' labor group, the two women representatives, and the headmaster of the village school. Supported by their community, this group found funding sources and organized the construction and management of an improved well.[4]

Each of these situations involves a common problem: How do residents of an area "build community?" How do they:

- develop and sustain strong relationships?
- increase problem-solving and group decision-making skills?
- improve their ability to collaborate effectively to identify goals and get work done?

How, in other words, do they develop their capacity to blend with other resources to accomplish important tasks, such as attracting new businesses, renovating homes, energizing schools, or reclaiming a burnt and abandoned block?

Citizens who demand more control of their lives, elected officials scrambling to undo decades of urban deterioration, foundation officers seeking the best way to distribute resources—all are asking similar questions about the best ways to "build community."

Our Search for Critical Factors

What leads to successful community building? What distinguishes efforts that succeed from those that fail? Motivated by these questions, our goal is to describe what we know—from the research literature—about community building. We want to:

- Provide a helpful tool for community residents, leaders, and funders who wish to develop their communities in ways that will result in other improvements—whether social, economic, housing, health, educational, safety, or other.
- Publish a reference that reports on and synthesizes what research tells us about community building strategies.

---

[4] This case was summarized from "Community Participation and Rural Water Supply Development in Sierra Leone" by O. M. Bah.

In recent years, many have lamented a possible loss of community in developed nations. Politicians, nonprofit groups, funders, schools, and community residents alike have cited the importance of building community. Yet little agreement exists on how to focus attention on "community" (with its many definitions) or on what factors are most important in building it. Research has been conducted on these topics, but no single publication synthesizes this work in a way that can easily be used by community residents, funders, policy makers, and others who want to select the best ways to improve communities. Many people involved in community building and its funding have asked for a practical, research-based compendium of information that can make them more efficient and effective in their work.

Michael Patton, noted evaluation expert, observes that a major challenge of our Information Age is to keep up with, sort, absorb, and *use* all the information available to us. He contends that "in the fields of nutrition, energy conservation, education, criminal justice, financial investment, human services, corporate management, international development—the list could go on and on—a central problem, often *the* central problem, is getting people to apply what is already known." (Patton 1997) The need to understand and apply what we have already learned exists in the field of community building as strongly as in most other fields.

This book helps to meet the need to take a look across initiatives for common lessons in community building. The thousands of hours of preparation required for this book (identifying research, assessing its quality, gauging its fit with our goals, learning what it has to say, and grouping findings together to reach conclusions) is the nitty-gritty homework that all of us who are interested in community building rarely have the time to do. The resulting product offers practical information, based on research, to enable us to build community more effectively and efficiently. In addition, it can enable us, as Stone[5] writes, to "think, question, discuss, and debate" our efforts.

---

[5] Rebecca Stone of the Chapin Hall Center for Children at the University of Chicago contends that: the field of community building "has not taken full advantage of this growth in practice to look across initiatives for common lessons, or to delve into fundamental issues that bear on all efforts in community change, and so to strengthen its understanding of how distressed communities can (or why they should) coordinate their resources to effect positive change. Many in the field complain that there is no time to stop and think, question, discuss, and debate the nature of the enterprise, but this kind of reflection is sorely needed . . ."

Our Method

To develop this report, we identified all the written evaluation research literature we could find on community building—all told, some 525 studies. We included and inspected research conducted on any activities undertaken to strengthen communities, catalogued under a variety of terms, such as community development, community building, and community empowerment.[6] We developed a set of criteria to sort the literature according to its quality and its relevance for our goals. We eliminated those studies that did not meet our criteria, resulting in a final pool of forty-eight studies.

We reviewed this final pool of studies, mostly case studies, for key ingredients that resulted in the success (or failure) of specific community building initiatives. These key ingredients from all the individual studies were then combined into a list of factors that are described in Chapters Two and Three. (A complete description of our methods can be found in Appendix B.)

Sharpening Our Focus

Our topic is immense. To develop a useful document for people interested in the real-world labor of actually strengthening communities—not just talking about it—we had to sharpen our focus. We accomplished this in the following ways:

1. We focused on one type of community—probably the most common type: communities formed on the basis of where people live.

2. We focused on the building of community strengths that relate to social capacity or social readiness to accomplish tasks or improve community living standards.

3. We focused only on the ways that community building initiatives increase those strengths—not on the other matters that influence those strengths.

4. We focused on social capacity—a community's internal potential to accomplish what it needs to do; we didn't focus on task accomplishment itself.

5. We defined certain terms to make our analysis uniform across different studies.

"I would rather discover a single fact, even a small one, than debate the great issues at length without discovering anything at all."

— Galileo Galilei

---

[6] Appendix A describes many of these terms.

Focusing on the Communities "Where People Live"

People use the term *community* in a variety of ways. The popular press often uses phrases like "the community of Des Moines," or "the business community." We refer to "the Hispanic community," or "the Jewish community," or other ethnic communities. In the Information Age, even users of the Internet are sometimes deemed a "community."

Researchers of community building have no standard definition of community. Therefore, our first task as a research team was to establish a working definition of community—one that would be concrete and uniform enough to have a focus, yet broad enough to serve a variety of situations. We found close to twenty-five definitions in the publications we reviewed. We also spoke with practitioners and other researchers about the many definitions of community. (Descriptions of many of these definitions appear in Appendix A.)

After studying the various definitions, we decided to focus on the following type of community:

> *People who live within a* **geographically defined area** *and who have* **social and psychological ties** *with each other and with the place where they live.*[7]

The definition of this type of community has two important components:

1. An emphasis on place: It applies to people who live within a specific area.[8]

   Our definition focuses attention on communities that most people would characterize as "residential." If asked where *home* is, you would most likely think of your house or apartment, the block you live on, and the larger neighborhood that surrounds you. This is why our definition of community includes aspects of place and the psychological and social ties to that place. We believe our definition is one that most people accept as common sense. It can easily include urban neighborhoods, small towns, or other areas that people identify as the place where they live, or as their "home."

2. A focus on social and psychological ties: In our working definition, it is the existence of social and psychological ties that constitutes the essence of community.

---

[7] Of the definitions listed in Appendix A, this is most similar to the definition used by Christenson and Robinson (1989).

[8] This area could, in theory, be any size; but practically, it is typically restricted to areas that one would commonly perceive as an urban neighborhood or a small rural town.

Social ties include interactions based on kinship, friendship, and familiarity with other people within a geographic area, as well as joint participation in community-wide activities and some forms of economic exchange (purchasing goods and services, working for local employers, and so forth).

Psychological ties include feelings of attachment, identity, and a sense of belonging to a place, as well as a sense of commitment, respect, obligation, and camaraderie with fellow occupants of that place.

Obviously, our definition does not include many types of social networks that people consider communities. In fact, many of the reviewers of this document noted that our definition does not cover communities of identity (for example, the Black community, the Gay community), communities of profession (for example, the sports community, the business community), and communities of faith (for example, the Baptist community, or the Muslim community). The definition also does not capture communities based solely on kinship or friendship.

All these types of communities are very important, but to include them would have caused us to cast too broad a net. We would have been less able to focus on our goal of identifying effective strategies in community building. In addition, we would have strayed from the most usual sense in which people use community, especially people who seek to revitalize troubled neighborhoods.[9]

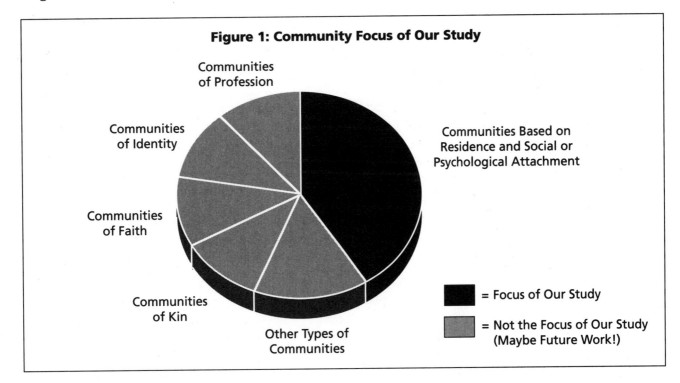

Figure 1: Community Focus of Our Study

Communities of Profession

Communities of Identity

Communities of Faith

Communities of Kin

Other Types of Communities

Communities Based on Residence and Social or Psychological Attachment

■ = Focus of Our Study

▨ = Not the Focus of Our Study (Maybe Future Work!)

---

[9] Depending upon the usefulness of the present work, we may expand our efforts to review research related to these other types of communities. Or, if we can't get to it, we encourage other researchers to do so!

Focusing on Social Strengths

After deciding on the types of communities to which we would devote attention, we had to set up procedures to help us distinguish research that pointed to improved community building, as opposed to research that related to other aspects of community status or functioning. Therefore, we decided to focus on the building of community strengths that relate to *social* capacity or *social* readiness to accomplish tasks or improve community living standards.

We have chosen the term *community social capacity*[10] to refer to a community's ability to work together in concert. (Other authors have referred to this capability of communities by use of such terms as *assets, capacity*, and *social capital*.) Communities with high social capacity can successfully identify problems and needs; achieve a workable consensus on goals and priorities; agree on how to pursue goals; and cooperate to achieve goals. These abilities or competencies exist, to some degree, in most communities. The research reviewed for this report relates to the factors that influence this capacity.

Focusing on Community Building Initiatives

Community building initiatives, for purposes of this work, are any identifiable set of activities pursued by a community in order to increase the so-

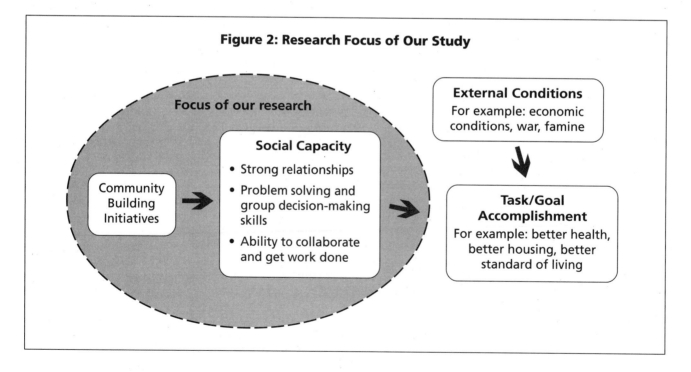

Figure 2: Research Focus of Our Study

Focus of our research

Community Building Initiatives

Social Capacity
- Strong relationships
- Problem solving and group decision-making skills
- Ability to collaborate and get work done

External Conditions
For example: economic conditions, war, famine

Task/Goal Accomplishment
For example: better health, better housing, better standard of living

---

[10] We base our use of the term *community social capacity* on a related definition proposed by Cottrell (1976).

cial capacity of its members. These activities can be initiated either as a result of a decision within the community or as a result of some effort outside the community. The goal of our research, as stated earlier, is to identify what factors lead to the success of these initiatives, which constitute, in the words of John Gardner (1993), "the practice of building connections among residents, and establishing positive patterns of individual and community behavior based on mutual responsibility and ownership."

Focusing on Social Capacity, Not on Task Accomplishment

Task and goal accomplishment refer to the activities a community must perform in order to meet the day-to-day requirements of life, as well as to achieve optimal physical, social, mental, and environmental well-being. The accomplishment of tasks and goals probably depends on many factors: sweeping economic and social trends (economic recession, increase in the aging population); broad-based political forces (increased centralization or decentralization in government); and environmental forces (war, earthquakes); as well as on the social capacity of a community.

Thus, it is very important to note that task and goal accomplishment are *not* the outcomes of a community building process. The outcomes of community building efforts are an improved *capacity* to accomplish tasks and goals and a heightened sense of community—a strengthening of social and psychological ties to the place and to other residents, not the actual accomplishment of goals.

Our work separates the *building* of community from the ultimate accomplishment of critical tasks and goals. Community social capacity constitutes one of a variety of resources that offer communities the *potential* to get things accomplished.

Other researchers and practitioners have also made this important conceptual distinction. For example, using slightly different terms, the Committee for Economic Development (1995) asserted the importance of "social capital" as a precondition for addressing community problems:

> Social capital is the attitudinal, behavioral, and communal
> glue that holds society together through relationships among
> individuals, families, and organizations. Without social
> capital . . . efforts to address specific problems of individuals,
> families, and neighborhoods will make little progress.

Although a community with high social capacity may have an increased likelihood of improving its quality of life, community social capacity is not the sole determinant of quality of life. External forces (economic, social, political, environmental) have a strong influence. For example, the livelihood of even the most well-functioning community is heavily affected by forces totally (or almost totally) out of its control, such as wars, droughts, or criminal activities by perpetrators from the outside.

The importance of external forces becomes very evident as we attempt to strengthen communities in the United States. Effective community action relies in part on a strong economic base. External economic conditions (employment, inflation rates, the value of the dollar on world markets) influence the economic base of communities throughout the United States, but no single community is in a position to influence them.

Research relevant for our examination—consistent with this idea—is research that examines the link between a specific community building process and community social capacity. From this research, we can identify critical ingredients that lead from whatever activities a community attempts to a resulting increase in community social capacity.

Note that much of the work done under the rubric of "community development" involves projects intended to improve community well-being through some tangible accomplishment (for example, building a dam to improve the energy supply or enhance land use; developing improved street lighting to improve safety). The more often that these projects include a community building component, the greater the likelihood of success with an overall community building initiative. Kincaid and Knop (1992:4) exhort those interested in community building to understand this as a "basic, practical lesson":

> In addition to tangible project goals and citizen learning experiences, general project goals should include attention to building a sense of community, opening up local participation, and encouraging a realistically optimistic view of the community's future among a broad range of citizens.

Some Important Terms

In this report, we try to use several terms consistently, in order to avoid confusion. These are the terms:

Leaders (of a community building initiative): The leaders of a community building initiative are those people who assume roles managing or directing an entire initiative, components of an initiative, specific tasks, or specific functions. Leaders, in our definition, always live within the community.

Organizers: The people who design, implement, and manage the community building process. They may be people from inside, or come from outside, the community.

Community social capacity: The extent to which members of a community can work together effectively. (See the longer description on pages 8-9.)

Community building: any identifiable set of activities pursued by a community in order to increase community social capacity.

Limitations of This Method

As a review of the existing research literature on community building, this publication has certain limitations. First, we could only use information that was written and available. We looked far and wide for written materials that could provide us with the kind of information that met our goals and qualified as good research. We scoured the country looking for published resources, and we contacted experts for their knowledge of available literature. However, most certainly, we missed some studies and couldn't acquire others.

Second, the questions asked by other researchers limited the scope of information available to us. For example, in recent years, some people have devoted attention to community building approaches that first, inventory community assets and strengths; and then, assemble specific plans to build on these positive community features. However, very few research studies have gathered information on the effectiveness of this strategy, so it could not enter our analysis.

Third, most of the available studies of community building are case studies. This limited what we could do. The case-study methodology typically includes limited statistical data, which means study findings can be interpreted in a variety of ways. We took precautions to minimize misinterpretations by doing multiple readings with multiple readers. Even so, it is possible that our interpretation of a study differed from the author's intention.

How This Book Is Organized

This chapter introduces readers to the rationale and basic method of our work. In Chapter Two, we briefly introduce each of the factors which emerged as important in our review of research. Chapter Three fully describes each factor, provides examples, and explains why the factor is important. Chapter Four offers some suggestions of practical implications for groups interested in community building. The Appendices explain our methodology and offer helpful resources.

Ways to Use This Book

We have mentioned audiences who may find this publication useful. Community leaders without much background in community building may find this a useful tool to bring them up to speed on important factors that influence the success of community building. Community development experts may find this useful to remind them of the important ingredients for success. Funders may see this publication as a tool to assess the ongoing work in communities in which they have invested. Researchers, we hope, will become aware of information needs that exist and will work to develop stronger ways to assess and evaluate community building initiatives.

Some ways this book may be useful are:

1. **For general understanding**. Developing a general understanding of the factors that are important in successful community building efforts is useful when considering strategies for working with communities.

2. **To apply to specific situations**. If you are involved in a community building effort, you might want to use the material in the following ways.

   - Use the success factors in Chapter Two as a checklist to determine if your initiative has the necessary components.

   - Use the content of Chapters Two and Three to expand your thinking about ways to help your community building effort to succeed.

   - After you have a community building effort under way, return to the material in the report to ask: What should we be watching out for? Are there changes we need to make?

Chapter Four discusses in more detail some ways you can use this book.

Chapter Two
Overview

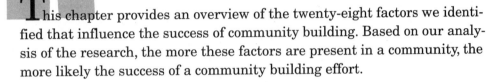

This chapter provides an overview of the twenty-eight factors we identified that influence the success of community building. Based on our analysis of the research, the more these factors are present in a community, the more likely the success of a community building effort.

We have divided these factors into three categories:

1. *Characteristics of the Community.* These are the social, psychological, and geographical attributes of a community and its residents that contribute to the success of a community building effort.

2. *Characteristics of the Community Building Process.* These are factors that make up the process by which people attempt to build community, such as representation, communications, and technical assistance.

3. *Characteristics of Community Building Organizers.* These factors are the qualities of those people who organize and lead a community building effort, such as commitment, trust, understanding, and experience.

A brief description of each of the twenty-eight factors follows. In-depth descriptions of the factors, along with examples and practical applications of the factors, appear in Chapter Three.

1. Characteristics of the Community

1A. Community Awareness of an Issue

Successful efforts more likely occur in communities where residents recognize the need for some type of initiative. A community building effort must address an issue that is important enough to warrant attention, and which affects enough residents of a community to spark self-interest in participation.

1B. Motivation from within the Community

Successful efforts more likely occur in communities where the motivation to begin a community building process is self-imposed, rather than encouraged from the outside.

1C. Small Geographic Area

Successful efforts are more likely to occur in communities with smaller geographic areas where planning and implementing activities are more manageable.

1D. Flexibility and Adaptability

Successful efforts are more likely to occur in communities where organized groups and individuals exhibit flexibility and adaptability in problem solving and task accomplishment.

1E. Preexisting Social Cohesion

Other things being equal, the higher the existing level of social cohesion (that is, the strength of interrelationships among community residents), the more likely a community building effort will be successful.

1F. Ability to Discuss, Reach Consensus, and Cooperate

Successful efforts tend to occur more easily in communities that have a spirit of cooperation and the ability to discuss openly their problems and needs.

1G. Existing Identifiable Leadership

Successful community building efforts are more likely when there are at least some residents who most community members will follow and listen to, who can motivate and act as spokespersons, and who can assume leadership roles in a community building initiative.

1H. Prior Success with Community Building

Communities with prior positive experience with community building efforts are more likely to succeed with new efforts.

2. Characteristics of the Community Building Process

2A. Widespread Participation

Successful efforts occur more often in communities that promote widespread participation.

2B. Good System of Communication

Successful community building efforts tend to have well-developed systems of communication.

2C. Minimal Competition in Pursuit of Goals

Successful efforts tend to occur in communities where existing community organizations do not perceive other organizations or the leaders of a community building initiative as competitors.

2D. Develop Self-Understanding

Successful efforts are more likely to occur when the process includes developing a group identity, clarifying priorities, and agreeing on how to achieve goals.

2E. Benefits to Many Residents

Successful efforts are more likely if community goals, tasks, and activities have clear, visible benefits to many people in the community.

2F. Focus on Product and Process Concurrently

Community building initiatives are more likely to succeed when efforts to build relationships (the process focus) include tangible events and accomplishments (the product focus).

2G. Linkage to Organizations Outside the Community

Successful efforts are more likely to occur when members have ties to organizations outside the community.

2H. Progression from Simple to Complex Activities

Successful community building efforts are more likely when the process moves community members from simple to progressively more complex activities.

2I. Systematic Gathering of Information and Analysis of Community Issues

Successful community building efforts more likely occur when the process includes taking careful steps to measure and analyze the needs and problems of the community.

2J. Training to Gain Community Building Skills

Successful community building efforts more likely occur when participants receive training to increase their community building skills.

2K. Early Involvement and Support from Existing, Indigenous Organizations

Successful community building efforts tend to occur most often in situations where community organizations of long tenure and solid reputation become involved early.

2L. Use of Technical Assistance

Successful efforts more likely occur when community residents use technical assistance (experts providing consultation or hands-on training in their area of knowledge) to help residents gain competence in a particular area.

2M. Continual Emergence of Leaders, as Needed

Successful community building efforts more likely occur when the process includes the means to produce new leaders over time.

2N. Community Control Over Decision Making

Successful community building efforts more likely occur when residents have control over decisions, particularly over how funds are used.

2O. The Right Mix of Resources

Successful community building efforts occur when the process is not overwhelmed by too many resources or stifled by too few, and when there is a balance between internal and external resources.

3. Characteristics of Community Building Organizers

3A. Understanding the Community

Successful community building efforts tend to have organizers who have a thorough understanding of the culture, social structure, demographics, political structure, and issues in the community.

3B. Sincerity of Commitment

Successful community building efforts more likely occur when organized by individuals who convey a sincere commitment for the community's well-being.

3C. A Relationship of Trust

Successful efforts are more likely to occur when the organizers develop trusting relationships with community residents.

3D. Level of Organizing Experience

Successful community building efforts more likely occur when the organizers are experienced in the many facets of working with communities.

3E. Able to be Flexible and Adaptable

Successful community building efforts are more likely when the organizers are flexible and able to adapt to constantly changing situations and environments.

Chapter Three
Factors Related to Success

In this chapter, we describe the significant factors that influence the success of community building—factors identified through our synthesis of the research literature. Most studies of community building efforts are case studies, in which researchers describe one or more communities, provide an account of the community building activities these communities tried, and assess the level of success of these activities. In these studies, the researchers typically suggest the factors that led to success and cite evidence to support the importance of these factors.

We identified all the factors suggested in the literature, determined how strong the evidence appeared in support of each one, and developed a final list.[11] We then classified the factors into three groups:

1. Characteristics of the Community

2. Characteristics of the Community Building Process

3. Characteristics of Community Building Organizers

This chapter describes each factor within each of the three categories. Our logic is: the more that these factors are present, the more likely that a community building effort will succeed. In addition, we use the factor to raise some practical questions for people involved in community building efforts. We hope these questions will help you, as a reader interested in community building, cross the bridge from research to real-life situations.

[11] Approximately 525 studies were initially reviewed. As a result of screening, 48 of these were ultimately used in our analysis. Our method for reviewing and screening studies and for extracting the success factors from the literature is described in detail in Appendix B.

1. Characteristics of the Community

Characteristics of the community in which a community building effort takes place comprise one set of factors related to success. These factors include social and psychological attributes of the residents of the community. The more that these factors are present in a community, the greater the likelihood of success.

1A. Community Awareness of an Issue

Successful efforts more likely occur in communities where residents recognize the need for some type of initiative. A community building effort must address an issue which is important enough to warrant attention, and which affects enough residents of a community to spark self-interest in participation. The residents must know that the problem or issue exists.

Perception of a problem or an issue catalyzes groups.[12] It heightens interest; it motivates initial participation; and it sustains motivation as time goes by, or as challenges become great.

Simply speaking, community residents have many things to do. A community building initiative competes with existing obligations and inclinations. It may also create some risks. A community building initiative will only reach priority status among residents if they perceive a likely payoff. An initiative will more likely reach its goals if it promises positive change or the resolution of an issue of significant importance to most community residents.

Eisen (1994:241) noted that, in the seventeen initiatives she studied, all of which took shape between 1978 and 1990, "A strongly perceived threat to residents' well-being catalyzed the initial organization of the most effective empowerment initiatives, Dudley Street in Boston, Keysville in Georgia, and ROCC in Massachusetts."

Nationally and internationally, the same types of problems have motivated community residents to participate in community building efforts. These include the need for housing or shelter, community safety, threats to natural resources, concerns about health or fears of disease, and concerns about the future of a community's children.

---

[12] Professor Harold Hill, main character of *The Music Man,* well recognized the need for a problem to exist before community residents will coalesce to take action. Therefore, he created "trouble with a capital T, that rhymes with P, that stands for *pool!*"

Questions for Community Builders

- Are the objectives for our community building project based on the immediate concerns of the neighborhood? Can we broaden them later into a more comprehensive effort?[13]

- Do community members understand—and are they aware of—how the issues affect them?

1B. Motivation from within the Community

Successful efforts more likely occur in communities where the motivation to begin a community building process is self-imposed, rather than encouraged from the outside. In addition, the process seems to be more effective if ideas for goals and activities come from residents themselves.

Community "self-motivation" engenders widespread participation (an important factor noted in the next section). When ideas come from a community itself, the ability to accomplish tasks tends to increase.

A good example of the value of motivation from within is the work Meredith Minkler (1997) and others have done in the poverty-ridden Tenderloin District of San Francisco. There, community organizers worked with elderly in single room occupancy hotels to increase community members' abilities to address important issues. At first, the organizers went into the community uninvited to help residents organize and develop solutions to issues they wanted to address. The organizers found that they ended up in the role of service provider. As the project progressed, organizers determined that if they waited until resident groups requested organizing services such as leadership training they were "more effective in fostering true community organizing and empowerment."

Questions for Community Builders

- Does motivation already exist in our community?

- Do people in our community have the interest to work together to address an issue?

- Do the goals and tasks in our community building effort come directly from community members?

---

[13] Eisen (1994) makes this suggestion in her article.

1C. Small Geographic Area

Successful efforts are more likely to occur in communities with smaller geographic areas where planning and implementing activities are more manageable. Developing the relationships necessary for successful community building requires interaction. This interaction is harder to achieve if individuals are separated from one another by a great distance. In addition, activities which participants in a community building process may wish to accomplish are often more feasible if planned for a smaller area.

Davis (1991:147) discusses how urban renewal reduced the size of one neighborhood and consequently enabled the West End community in Cincinnati to organize with greater ease.[14]

> The combined effect of highway construction and urban renewal concentrated fewer people into half the territorial space. The West End no longer contained sixty to seventy thousand people, covering some eight hundred acres of land. Nor did the neighborhood contain as many churches, stores, bars, parks, or clubs. Consequently, the people who remained in the West End interacted within a smaller physical space and shared more of the same social spaces. Such physical and social proximity was to make it easier for the neighborhood to share information and to develop a common sense of its own identity and interests.

Questions for Community Builders

- Is the focus for our activity within a defined and manageable geographic area?

- Do the people we are working with consider themselves part of the same community?

1D. Flexibility and Adaptability

Successful efforts more likely occur in communities where organized groups and individuals exhibit flexibility and adaptability in problem solving and task accomplishment.

A flexible community group remains open to a variety of ways to deal with issues. The residents have the inclination to do whatever is best, not simply whatever has been done in the past. This attribute ensures that progress on community building will not be deterred by such things as

---

[14] This renewal effort created a natural experiment within which to observe the importance of this factor.

allegiance to outdated or ineffective rules for performance, conformance to outmoded standards for technology, or other dysfunctional norms and practices.

An adaptable community group can shift goals and tasks as new needs arise—if such a shift will serve the ultimate goal of building community. Kincaid and Knop (1992:5) describe the importance of the ability of participants in a community building initiative to "redirect their efforts without recriminations" when activities are not working as hoped.[15]

Questions for Community Builders

- Are community members open to change?
- Do community norms place rigid restrictions on the methods of a community building process? Are there ways to remove or lessen these restrictions?
- Can we switch tasks, goals, or objectives if necessary?
- Are we stuck thinking about the issues or the process of community building in one way?

1E. Preexisting Social Cohesion

Other things being equal, the higher the existing level of social cohesion (that is, the strength of interrelationships among community residents), the more likely that a community building effort will be successful.

Communities that have a stable population, where people are not continually moving in and out, tend to have more success building community.

High social cohesion is related to a common spirit of problem solving, good communication, and a larger number of associational groups (civic, recreational, business, and so forth) in the community. In short, cohesive communities are already partly built. They tend to have structures that enhance the attributes identified by the literature as necessary for success (for example, trust and communication[16]). It is easier to increase the level of social capacity of these communities than it is to increase the social capacity of a community that has few preexisting social ties.

---

[15] They also note the balance necessary between "stick-to-it-ive-ness" and adaptability. That is, many tasks present great challenges and consume much energy and patience. Participants in an initiative need to discern between tasks for which they should persist, because success will probably occur, and tasks which are simply not feasible or not appropriate, and which they should discontinue.

[16] These characteristics are listed in the next sections.

Questions for Community Builders

- Is there a stable population of people to work with, or are people continuously moving in and out?

- Do organizations or associational groups (religious, sports, business, other) operate effectively in the community? Can they be tapped as a resource for community building efforts?

- Are there particular groups in the community that are not well connected? Are there ways to strengthen the interrelationships among these groups so all residents can participate more fully?

- Do any commonly held values among community members offer a basis for building cohesion (for example, the desire for better health services or education)?

1F. Ability to Discuss, Reach Consensus, and Cooperate

Successful efforts tend to occur more easily in communities that have a spirit of cooperation and the ability to discuss openly their problems and needs. Members of such communities may not necessarily have formally solved problems together, but they have had a history of coming together to help neighbors during a crisis or of working together on social or religious events. In addition, if a community has previously solved common problems, or even been involved in previous community building efforts, this experience is likely to have enhanced the ability of residents to work together in the future.

This spirit was notable for its absence in a rural community in Oregon that had received community-organizing assistance for many years. Declining economics in the community made it eligible for many services and programs. Research, planning, and discussions had been ongoing in the community for about seven years without any changes. Researchers determined that a variety of forces affected the lack of change. First, the people in the community had been socialized not to disagree publicly, so it was hard to have a meaningful discussion. Second, in the past, any suggestions of change had been met with strong private criticism, so people were hesitant to bring creative ideas to the table. Finally, there was such a strong tradition of individualism in the community that members could not openly discuss problems, because they did not believe in collective effort as a way to solve problems. (Hibbard, 1986)

Questions for Community Builders

- Do the people in this community have a history of working together to solve problems or help people?

- Do any activities offer community members the opportunity to practice open dialogue, develop trust, and increase group decision-making skills?[17]

1G. Existing Identifiable Leadership

Successful efforts more likely occur in communities with existing, identifiable leadership. That is, they tend to occur in communities containing at least some residents who most community members will follow and listen to, who can motivate and act as spokespersons, and who can assume leadership roles in a community building initiative.

In many of the initiatives reported in the research, a local leader, or set of leaders, lit the spark that brought about the initiative. For example, one study surveyed forty-one community organizations and asked, "What caused the organization's creation? Who or what was the main source of support in the creation?" The answer to this question was that the community organizations were started by individuals with a view of a problem, or problems, and ideas of what had to be done in order to begin to solve them. (The National Commission on Neighborhoods, 1979)

In some communities, local leadership is available, but it gets spread too thinly to be effective. An example of this occurred in the West End of Cincinnati during the 1970's, where the Black community leadership was pulled in many directions.

> The council's leadership was slowly enfeebled by several factors, some structural and some personal. First, the proliferation of organizational commitments simply spread neighborhood leadership far too thinly. In the early sixties, the community council had little competition from other locality-based organizations for the small supply of talented, ambitious, civic-minded individuals with leadership ability that most neighborhoods contain. Ten years later, the community council was not the "only game in town" for West End blacks. There were a half-dozen block clubs in the upper West End and Queensgate II; there were resident councils in each of the public housing projects; there were the West End Health Center, and the Arts consortium; there was the West End Credit

---

[17] Hibbard (1986) suggested this approach in his article.

union; there were a dozen neighborhood representatives on the West End Task Force; and there were ten representatives from the West End on the Resident Neighborhood Community Association of Model Cities. Then too, nearly every federal program that served the West End had its own requirement for "Citizen participation," placing additional demands on the limited time of the neighborhood's leadership. (Davis, 1991:163-164)

Questions for Community Builders

- Does the community have members who are already taking on visible leadership positions (scout leaders, religious leaders, people who organize community events)? Are these people available and interested in doing additional community building?

- Does the community have a reservoir of leadership, as yet overlooked, in the form of leaders such as Head Start parents or block-watchers?

- What would it take to involve and train people who have not taken on leadership positions in the past?

1H. Prior Success with Community Building

Communities with prior positive experience with community building efforts are more likely to succeed with new efforts. This factor was of particular importance in the international studies. Communities with prior negative experiences were more wary of the process; they had been disappointed in the past by development and government agencies that started community building efforts but did not follow through or undermined the process in some way. This made it particularly difficult to initiate new efforts.

Questions for Community Builders

- Does this community have a history of working with community building? Was it a successful experience?

- If it was unsuccessful, what needs to be done to increase trust and confidence in the present community building process?

- If the community has no experience, what is the best way to get started, taking some small steps, rather than moving immediately into a full-grown initiative?

2. Characteristics of the Community Building Process

Characteristics of the process used to accomplish a community building effort comprise a second set of factors related to success. Many different activities may produce the same results. What is important is that these activities have the characteristics noted in this section. The more that these factors are present in a community building process, the greater the likelihood of success.

2A. Widespread Participation

Without a doubt, successful efforts occur more often in communities that promote widespread participation in the community building process. This participation must be:

> *Representative*—that is, the community building process includes members of all, or most, segments of the community at any specific point in time.

> *Continuous*—that is, the community building process recruits new members over time, as some members leave for one reason or another.

Representative participation provides strength to a community building effort because:

- It brings the talents and resources of a wider, more diverse group of individuals into the process. This is especially important for problem solving and task accomplishment.

- It increases the likelihood of political acceptability of any activities, programs, or policies that grow from the community building effort.

- It increases the likelihood of ties to outsiders who may have resources to contribute or who may control elements of the environment that can affect the success of the community's effort.

Participation at all levels of an initiative, from policy to task accomplishment, appears important. Successful efforts build in ways to involve as many community members as possible. An example illustrates the point. At Banana Kelly, a Bronx-based community development corporation, participation among previously homeless residents in a housing program was mandatory.

The families were required to participate in weekly group meetings designed to help them to begin taking responsibility for their living space and lives. Officers were elected, and residents were required to identify and develop solutions for problems which arose in the building. Further, they were given significant authority in the management of the building, including screening prospective tenants and hiring janitors. The program has catalyzed strong support among tenants for conformance with rules the residents themselves promulgated and now enforce. (Leiterman and Stillman, 1993:31)

An elected board that represents all constituencies in a community can often serve as one route to representative participation. In *Streets of Hope*, Peter Medoff and Holly Sklar (1994:57) describe the outcome of a detailed process to structure a board to ensure resident control and representation. At first, the twenty-three member governing board was organized to include only four spots for community members. The community did not feel this was fair, so a new organizational structure was developed. The new structure included a thirty-one member board with a resident majority. In addition "equal minimum representation was provided for the neighborhood's four major cultures–Black, Cape Verdean, Latino, and White–rather than representation based simply numerically on Dudley's population. Equal minimum representation was chosen to strengthen collective action and underscore the common stake of all people in rebuilding Dudley."

While representation must be widespread, continuous recruitment is also critical. A steady stream of incoming new members—either to replace departing members or to supplement existing membership—helps sustain representative participation.

The need to plan for, and spend time on, the recruitment of new participants is often overlooked. Community building initiatives may begin with great energy and enthusiasm. Participants seem to represent all segments of the community, and the reservoir of skills and time they are willing to donate appears more than adequate to accomplish the necessary tasks.

However, the initiative may take months or years to complete. Attrition sets in. Normal events in the lives of participants—employment, family, and health status to name a few—produce expectable resignations from both volunteer assignments and paid positions.

The Dudley Street Neighborhood Initiative (DSNI) diligently recruits members and trains them in community organizing skills, so that a large number of people are ready to assume responsibility for tasks as needs arise, or as personnel turn over. According to their director, "We train everyone in DSNI, all staff and leaders, to see themselves as organizers." (Medoff and Sklar, 1994:261).

Achieving widespread participation can be an awesome challenge. As the chair of a residents group in Detroit indicated, "Even bringing together people who are the most affected and engaging them in some discussion has been difficult. Most see it as a waste of time and don't get involved. Perhaps they are scared that the consequences would be too harsh to bear."[18]

Nevertheless, achieving widespread participation is an important ingredient of success.[19]

Questions for Community Builders

- Do the people participating in the community building initiative represent the population? Are some groups of community members not involved? How will this affect problem solving and decision making?

- Do mechanisms exist to help new participants feel accepted and part of the process?

- Does enough energy go into ongoing recruitment and outreach?

- What options exist to reach out to groups not already involved?

---

[18] Elisabethe Mack, Chairperson of the Jeffries Homes Residents Empowerment Committee, Detroit, Michigan. Quoted in Stone 1996.

[19] Unfortunately, confusion can sometimes develop over the necessity of widespread participation in a community building effort, as a result of examples of successful community *task accomplishment* brought about solely through the efforts of a small group of people. For example, a community may need a new bridge or new paving of a roadway, and a small group of business people, on its own, does whatever is necessary to bring this improvement into the community. However, such task accomplishment is not "community building," or the development of social capacity, as we have defined it.

2B. Good System of Communication

Successful efforts tend to have well-developed systems of communication. This includes communication within the community itself, as well as between the community and the rest of the world. Communication fosters community residents' awareness, motivation, participation, innovation, problem solving, and ability to mobilize.

Good communication also ensures that residents know the rationale for an initiative, the plan, and what's been accomplished over time. It sustains the momentum of a community building process. Participants need to feel a sense of accomplishment and need to see some concrete results, or they will likely lose enthusiasm. Communication increases the participants' motivation by increasing their sense of efficacy, their self-esteem, and by providing other rewards and incentives to continue doing their part.

A study of community building in community development corporations by Leiterman and Stillman (1993:107) provides a wonderful example of how communication can sustain motivation. One community organized an event to raise money for a youth center. For each person who joined hands in a circle around a five-block area in the community, corporate and individual sponsors would donate money. Eight hundred people attended the event. According to the executive director of the project, "the success of the Hands Around Egleston Square event lay not only in the money raised, but perhaps more importantly in its demonstration to the community that action can lead to results."

Communication ensures that *all* segments of the community remain aware and motivated, serving to maintain the widespread participation earlier noted as an ingredient for success. It also fosters the generation of innovative ideas and problem solving, by convening many talents and resources to accomplish tasks large and small.

Communication also helps participants in a community building initiative assemble quickly when necessary. Often, community building efforts confront an unexpected obstacle or crisis—a shift in politics, an imminent funding cut, the loss of a key leader, or an attempt to derail the project. In such circumstances, communication can mean the difference between survival and extinction. Communication enables the leaders to quickly convey accurate information, to enlist help, to convene participants, and to assign the tasks necessary to deal with the obstacle.

Communication techniques that showed up in the case studies we examined include: festivals, parties, parades, newsletters, news releases, special events, public meetings, establishing neighborhood information brokers, and establishing networks with resource people.

Two particularly valuable examples of the worth of person-to-person communication come from the Annie E. Casey Foundation's "Plain Talk Program," a community approach to reducing teen pregnancy now underway in six cities around the country. A main component of the Plain Talk Program is a survey done in each city to map out the community's attitudes, behavior, and services. The cities had different strategies for communicating the findings of the surveys with varying success. San Diego and New Orleans both were successful in bringing members of the communities together to discuss findings and move on to the next steps.

In San Diego, community forums were held to present findings from their community surveys. The organizers posted notices and, using names collected during the survey, they personally contacted over six hundred people individually to get the word out to attend the forums. The forums were well attended and provided an opportunity for community members to learn more about the project and to discuss how to communicate better with teens. (Kotloff, Roaf, and Gambone, 1995)

The other example from the Casey project comes from a housing project in New Orleans. To inform community members of their study findings and increase participation in the project, organizers conducted Home Health Parties:

> They recruited the first hostesses from among resident members of the survey team that conducted community mapping, and who received training in leadership skills and community organization during the year. However, as the parties progressed, residents who had themselves attended a party, or who had heard positive reports from their neighbors, volunteered to be hostesses. Seventy-five of the eighty-eight parties were attended by women and hosted by community residents, each of whom was asked to invite six to eight family members and friends to discuss results of the community mapping surveys. (Kotloff, Roaf, and Gambone, 1995: 56-57)

Questions for Community Builders

- Does communication about community building activities occur in a timely way?

- Is communications a part of the overall community building process and not just an add-on responsibility?

- Does the community building effort have a variety of techniques and strategies to reach as many people as possible?

2C. Minimal Competition in Pursuit of Goals

Successful efforts tend to occur in communities where existing community organizations do not perceive other organizations or the leaders of a community building initiative as competitors.

The overall mission or purpose of a community building initiative needs to be acceptable to as many organizations as possible. This increases the willingness of organization members to participate in the initiative, and it promotes a collaborative spirit. However, organizations balk at participation in an effort where another organization takes on tasks that they consider their responsibility.

Communities that have duplication of activities by many organizations tend to deplete leadership and other resources in the community. Community building efforts have sometimes failed not because the elements for success weren't there, but because there was so much competition for resources and leadership talent.

Questions for Community Builders

- Do multiple community building efforts presently operate in the community? Do they have similar activities working with the same people? Is this a source of conflict?

- Are leadership and resources in this community building effort stretched because of competition between groups?

2D. Develop Self-Understanding

Successful efforts are more likely to occur when the process includes developing a group identity, clarifying priorities, and agreeing on how to achieve goals.

Successful community building efforts spend time creating a legal or conceptual identity. This task often brings out some of the issues most important to the community. Critical questions arise in developing an identity such as: (1) What is the purpose of the effort? (2) What geographical area does the effort represent? and (3) How do we want the wider community to view us? Developing a name and identity is sometimes the first task a group has to accomplish together. From the research, it appears that those able to arrive at consensus are able to move on to next steps; those unable to reach consensus have difficulty with other decisions as well.

Related to developing an identity are decisions about which issues are most important. In any community, many needs exist and there never seem to be enough resources to meet them. Resident groups have more success when they take time at the beginning of a process for each person to explicitly state his or her needs and then decide, as a group, which needs are most important.

After a decision on priorities, community members need to know what has to be done to accomplish activities. Timelines and breaking larger tasks down into smaller ones help to increase understanding of how long it takes to accomplish a task and what the steps are. A clear understanding of the steps can help sustain motivation and ward off frustration.

Questions for Community Builders

- Do community members agree on important aspects of their identity? Who they represent? What geographical area they represent? What their purpose is?
- Do community members have a clear understanding of priorities?
- Does a fair process exist for making decisions?
- Do group members know what steps need to occur to accomplish tasks and ultimately to reach goals?

2E. Benefits to Many Residents

Successful community building efforts occur more often when community goals, tasks, and activities have clear benefits to many people in the community, and when these benefits are visible. Communities that choose goals and activities that have the most benefits for the most people have wider participation and more sustained participation. In general, residents are more interested and enthusiastic.

Questions for Community Builders

- Do goals and activities reflect the needs of most members of the community?
- Do people in the community know about the benefits expected from the community building activities and goals?

2F. Focus on Product and Process Concurrently

Community building initiatives are more likely to succeed when efforts to build relationships (the process focus) include tangible events and accomplishments (the product focus). Work to build relationships, without any perceptible progress or visible signs of achievement for the community, tends to wear residents down. Communities that focus solely on leadership development and the social needs of the community, with no perceptible progress, quickly see their residents' participation rates drop.

A danger that communities can fall into occurs when a community building initiative comprises part of a larger development project. Often, people focus on the physical or economic development tasks, confusing them with tasks necessary for community building. In several cases cited in the literature, one particular person or group took over development projects, made decisions, and got a specific community improvement job done. However, this did not foster community building; it simply accomplished a task.

In an evaluation of the Colorado Rural Revitalization Project, community members were surveyed about the extent to which activities yielded practical community benefits. About 90 percent of the respondents stated that activities had yielded "somewhat" to a "great deal" of benefit for the community. Outcomes noted by citizens as important included, (a) gaining the ability to cooperate, work together, and organize effectively for community revitalization; and (b) increases in citizen awareness, participation, and commitment to community improvement, along with increases in local pride and "sense of community." (Kincaid and Knop, 1992:23)

Successful efforts tend to occur in situations where specific projects to improve the community also include activities to accomplish community building. The leaders continue over time to devote attention to community organizing, bringing new residents into the process, and training residents to organize the community.

Questions for Community Builders

- Is there a balance in our community building efforts between achieving ultimate goals and paying attention to the process?

- Do we have the funding available for the aspects of community building that are not tied to achieving goals?[20]

---

[20] Minkler (1992) makes this suggestion in her article. Also, see O'Donnell, et al.(1995).

2G. Linkage to Organizations Outside the Community

Successful efforts are more likely to occur when members have ties to organizations outside the community. Such ties produce at least the following benefits:

Financial input: Linkages offer a source of revenue for community building efforts.

Political support: Linkages can offer policy makers a better understanding of the needs of a community, as well as promote a kindred spirit between community residents and policy makers. This can prevent political decisions that might undo strong community relationships.

Source of knowledge: Linkages can offer a source of ideas through contacts, referrals to individuals, or reference sources. Community residents learn and gain motivation by watching their peers in other communities. Sometimes, community building projects described in the research literature had participants purposefully visit other communities. In other cases, simply the association of community members with people in other communities led naturally to the exchange of information. Such learning enables community residents to see the accomplishments of other communities, to see how other communities overcome barriers, and to apply this knowledge to their own situation. Evidence suggests that sharing information across communities occurs most effectively among communities with similar income, education, and sometimes ethnicity or culture.

Source of technical support: Linkages can offer a pipeline to expert help or material technology that can benefit a community building process.

Successful efforts tend to have leaders who are involved with people and activities in other communities. These leaders provide a communication and resource link to whatever else happens in a broader context. Community building efforts identified as successful in the research literature often built networks to prevent or reduce their isolation.

Davis (1991) discusses the work of one community leader in the West End of Cincinnati:

> Mallory, a West End native residing in Park Town, was thirty-one years old when he became president of the West End Community Council. A natural politician, he spent the next three years cultivating strong vertical ties between the council and various officials and agencies in the city administration, while building the council's horizontal base in the West End.

Questions for Community Builders

- Do community members have formal or informal links to people and organizations in government and other communities? If not, can they develop these links?

- Should people from outside the community be invited to join in the community building effort (for example, as members of a board or an advisory committee)?

- Do we have efforts going on to build relationships with outside agencies, political officials, the media, and funders as we are building relationships within the community?

- Have we examined other community building efforts like ours, so we can learn from them?

2H. Progression from Simple to Complex Activities

Successful community building efforts are more likely to occur when the process moves community members from simple to progressively more complex activities. In many examples described in the research literature, work started with a simple task such as a neighborhood cleanup or a community picnic. The leaders and other participants developed skills in making decisions, and practiced working together to solve problems. As group confidence increased with success on smaller projects, groups progressed to more complex tasks such as changing community ordinances or starting a community development corporation.

For example, in Pleasant City, Florida, organizers worked with citizens hoping to develop a Community Development Corporation in their community. They had no experience working, planning, making decisions, or communicating as a group. Organizers suggested that their first task be a town meeting to introduce the group to the community. The tasks were not hard to do but required cooperation. The group successfully organized the meeting, which provided experience and momentum for more complicated tasks. (Gittel, Vidal and Turner, 1994:21)

Questions for Community Builders

- Are the activities planned for this effort reasonable, given community members' ability to accomplish tasks?

- Does this community building effort have both long- and short-term goals as a way to develop community members' skills? [21]

21. Systematic Gathering of Information and Analysis of Community Issues

Successful community building efforts more likely occur when the process includes taking careful steps to measure and analyze the needs and problems of the community. Successful efforts devote time and resources to understanding problems and possible solutions. Gathering information is one way to involve people and is often used as a task in community building. People gain knowledge about the community as well as forge stronger relationships with other community members. The results of information gathering and analysis often provide a direction for how to proceed with the next steps.

For example, in Eldorado, Illinois, the community members gathered facts about themselves and found out many in the community had low-quality housing, often lacking running water or indoor toilets. By gathering the facts, community members could more honestly discuss problems. (Bruyn, 1963)

In Oakland, California, community members conducted a door-to-door health survey to gather facts about health needs in the community. The results showed that there were inadequate health services, lack of transportation to health facilities, massive underinsurance, a lack of trained multilingual personnel, and a 24 percent under-immunization rate. The survey results provided community members with a clear direction on how to proceed in their next steps—to campaign for free immunizations and multilingual personnel at the health department. (Delgado, 1993)

---

[21] See Gittel, Vidal, and Turner (1994).

Questions for Community Builders

- Does this community building effort have enough information about the issues in the community to take action?

- Would additional information about community issues help to direct discussions? Provide background for developing solutions? Assist in solving problems and developing consensus?

2J. Training to Gain Community Building Skills

Successful community building efforts are more likely to occur when participants receive training in the skills needed increase their community building skills. Some people refer to this as leadership training. Examples of such training topics include group facilitation skills, organizational skills, human relations skills, and skills in how to analyze complex community issues. This training may be self-directed; it may come from an outside specialist; or it may be delivered by a formal community organizer.

Training is an essential piece of many initiatives. It helps participants understand their problems and gives them the skills to make changes, so they are less reliant on government or other organizations.

In the examples we examined, training took the form of teaching, mentoring, coaching, and modeling. Sometimes it occurred one-on-one, as individuals were groomed for a particular task or role. Other times, training was a group event, in which the members learned together how to approach a problem or evaluate work that was done. An example of making education and training an integral part of the community building process comes from Helen Lewis's observations of Ivanhoe, Virginia:

> Education became the cornerstone of the community development activity in Ivanhoe, first informally and then intentionally to develop people's understanding and skills. . . . Members of the group also attended other conferences and workshops on community development, housing, community organizing, and leadership building. The task of learning how to develop and maintain an organization and enter the community development and economic planning process began.

> People learned a lot quickly in the development process. They learned informally through the various confrontations with local authorities. They also learned through the workshops and conferences and from consultants and various helpers who came to the community. [Local resident] Clyde Shinault assessed some of the informal education: "it's educated me on more than I have ever dreamed on local

government. Our local government over the years have just plain-out lied to us." But experience is not enough; people need to reflect and analyze, make connections, and understand how the experience is part of larger events. (Hinsdale, 1995:79-80)

An example of an ongoing process to ensure an adequate supply of community building skills among community residents is the ten-year-old Blandin Community Leadership Program. Nearly two thousand individuals have received training in this program, which strives "to cultivate and train a broad base of local leaders to work collaboratively in their home communities to anticipate change, manage conflict, build consensus, and envision the future." (Blandin Foundation, 1996)

Questions for Community Builders

- What training do participants need in this community building effort? How can it be obtained?

- Do participants see a need for training in a particular area? What would be most beneficial?

- Is training an ongoing part of the community building process (tasks, activities, meetings are considered a learning experience), or is it a one-time effort?

- Do experienced participants train new people?

2K. Early Involvement and Support from Existing, Indigenous Organizations

Successful community building efforts tend to occur most often in situations where community organizations of long tenure and solid reputation become involved early. Many community building efforts have been initiated or supported by religious congregations, civic groups, governmental agencies, and schools. This involvement brings:

Established contacts: Preexisting relationships provide channels of communication within a community, which, as we have already seen, are necessary for success.

Legitimization: The leaders of these organizations often act as opinion-leaders. Before deciding to participate, residents want to know these leaders' attitude toward an initiative. In some cases, approval by such leaders may be a necessary political step.

Access to resources: These organizations often have resources (for example, personnel, facilities, knowledge, equipment, ties to other organizations inside and outside the community) which a community building initiative can enlist.

Questions for Community Builders

- What organizations or groups in the community, such as religious congregations, parent-teacher groups, or business associations, have strong ties to the community?

- How can we recruit these groups to help with the community building effort?

2L. Use of Technical Assistance

Successful community building efforts are more likely to occur when community residents use technical assistance to gain necessary skills.

Technical assistance refers to experts providing knowledge and skills to community building efforts to supplement whatever community members lack. Sometimes, the technical assistance experts work both to impart knowledge and to train the participants to perform tasks themselves. Examples include strategic planning, board development, and group facilitation. In other cases, technical assistance experts help participants in a community building effort resolve a narrow technical problem, and they do not necessarily pass along these technical skills to the participants. Examples of acquiring this type of technical assistance include hiring researchers to design studies, using computer consultants to provide advice about computer systems, consulting with health experts to obtain data about a specific health problem, and contracting with fund raisers to write grants.

Technical assistance can increase the speed and efficiency of community building work. It can increase the quality of a community building effort with respect to planning, organizational development, and leadership development. Finally, the technical assistance provider often brings a helpful outside perspective into the process.

Questions for Community Builders

- Could we advance our community building process faster with the help of an outside expert?

- Do we want technical assistance experts to just provide information or a service, or do we want them to also be teachers?

- Will the technical experts we hire support our community building process?

2M. Continual Emergence of Leaders, as Needed

Successful community building efforts more likely occur when the processes produce new leaders over time. Leaders of community building efforts carry out instrumental activities, directing an entire process or a set of tasks, as well as morale-maintenance activities, such as rallying participants when necessary.

New leaders need to emerge over time for at least two reasons: first, to replace leaders who are leaving; and second, to fill new leadership roles in the community group or larger community. As the community building effort grows, there is an increasing need for people to take charge of different tasks.

The Tenderloin Senior Organizing Project (TSOP), a community building effort in downtown San Francisco, provides leadership training for many participants in the project. As part of this training, members participate in role playing prior to confrontations with landlords, city officials, and so forth. "Such exercises, and the selection and preparation of back-up leaders on any given issue, provide continuity should the primary leader be ill on the day of a planned action . . . and have enabled TSOP to develop a strong leadership cadre from among its membership." (Minkler 1997:118)

In a study of successful and unsuccessful block organizations, the authors found that block clubs that remained active were more likely to be able to replace leaders when necessary than block clubs that had ceased functioning. (Wandersman et al., 1985)

Community building efforts that encouraged participants to take leadership roles and were able to replace leaders when necessary were stronger than efforts that relied on one charismatic leader.

Questions for Community Builders

- Does this community building effort rely too heavily on the person who provided the spark for initiating the group?
- What needs does our effort have for leadership from multiple sources, and for leaders with different styles?[22]

---

[22] This is a suggestion from the *Woods Fund of Chicago, Evaluation of the Community Organizing Grant Program* (O'Donnell et al., 1995).

2N. Community Control Over Decision Making

Successful community building efforts more likely occur when residents have control over decisions, particularly over how funds are used. In the studies we examined, outside agencies—whether government or foundation—that provided funding or other resources often had their own agendas and requirements. Community groups that had control over the use of funds were able to be more autonomous, focusing their efforts more on their own needs as opposed to the agenda of an outside agency.

Successful groups were able to manage outside agendas and the agency staff without letting them derail the group's own desired purpose. External agencies often have their own agendas. Staff in those organizations may have the skills and experience to accomplish tasks much more efficiently and easily than a fledgling community group. The community building process can easily be co-opted by passionate outside agency staff. Unsuccessful groups were often pulled apart by the many purposes government and funding agencies placed upon them.

Questions for Community Builders

- Do we have the flexibility in this community building effort to make decisions about how best to use funds?

- What are the needs and agendas of our funders? Do they coincide with our needs?

2O. The Right Mix of Resources

Successful community building efforts occur when the process is not overwhelmed by too many resources or stifled by too few, and when there is a balance between internal and external resources.

The right mix of resources is essential. One dimension of this is the *source of resources*, internal versus external. A second dimension is the amount or *flow of resources*. Too much can overwhelm the community and doesn't allow for relationships or skills to develop. Too little can stifle any creativity or create barriers.

Source of resources: Successful efforts more likely occur in situations where community residents themselves put forth some of the funds necessary to finance the community building effort. The community members are more invested in the process because of their financial investment. Community residents are forced to use problem-solving skills and work on problems that are meaningful to them in an effort to raise funds and use internal resources. Those people who may be drawn to the process because of the possibility of financial gain lose interest, and people truly motivated to build community become stronger participants. A study from The National Commission on Neighborhoods found that grassroots organizations saw diversity of fund raising as important; however, raising funds from within the organization was also a necessary principle. Sixty-eight percent of the groups they studied raised some money from the community.

Flow of resources: People need resources to undertake even the simplest of processes. For example, to communicate with community members, one may need paper, a copy machine, and stamps and envelopes to recruit for a meeting. The lack of resources can influence the community's ability to carry out tasks which, in turn, will hamper its ability to develop competence.

Mindy Lieterman, in her report on community building by community development corporations, cites lack of resources as a barrier to community building. "The efforts we refer to as community building—the building and cultivation of relationships with residents and neighborhood and outside institutions—are severely undervalued and underfunded." (Leiterman and Stillman, 1993:68)

On the other hand, too many outside resources can be overwhelming and inhibit the work a community needs to develop community building skills. A study of eight rural development efforts found that the most successful efforts occur when "the financial resources are of an appropriate scale and are combined with solid planning, or are available gradually, so the community can slowly accumulate management experience." (Flora et al., 1993:27)

In Checkoway's study of a St. Louis urban neighborhood, the right mix also had to do with timing:

> Neighborhood leaders began their first project using voluntary donations and private resources. It was community crises, commitment, and leadership, not outside funding support, that gave them their start. . . . In time, neighborhood leaders developed their track record and received outside government funding, which allowed the Jeff-Vander-Lou Neighborhood to expand and diversify the program. Over time the community has benefited heavily from major private and public resources from outside the neighborhood. (Checkoway, 1985:261)

Questions for Community Builders

- Is the community building effort being overwhelmed by too many resources and not being allowed to build its internal strength?

- Is the community building effort at a point where it needs outside resources to grow?

- Does the community building effort include an investment of resources from within the community?

3. Characteristics of Community Building Organizers

Every community building effort has individuals who design, implement, and manage the effort. They may be people who live in the community, or they may be people from outside the community.

It is the characteristics of these individuals that comprise the third set of factors related to success. The more that these characteristics are present in organizers, the greater the likelihood of success.[23]

3A. Understanding the Community

Successful community building efforts more likely occur when organizers understand the community they serve. This includes an understanding of the community's culture, social structure, demographics, political structures, and issues. Our definition of these terms follows.

> *Culture*: the belief patterns, social norms, and significant traditions of community residents, such as religious and ethnic orientations, which influence the daily pattern of living and decision making.

> *Social structure*: the existing social networks of community residents (who talks with whom); which members assume which roles (instrumental roles related to task accomplishment, or support roles related to morale building).

> *Demographics*: the characteristics of the community's population, such as age groups, ethnicity, living arrangements, and housing patterns.

> *Political structures*: the formal and informal power relationships existing in the community.

> *Issues*: the major concerns on the minds of community residents.

Daley and Winter, in a study of Peace Corps volunteers in Ecuadorian villages, found that volunteers were more successful if they were more involved with the communities and had a better understanding of the individuals, structure, and customs. (Daley and Winter, 1978:74)

---

[23] Note that we use the term *organizer* in a very general sense, applying it to people who lead community building efforts. They may be paid staff or volunteers. They may be formally named, or they may have no special designation attached to them. We do not wish to imply that community building efforts always have a community organizer in any uniform or traditional sense of the term.

An individual's position as a community resident or nonresident may influence his or her understanding of the community, but it does not wholly determine this understanding. For example, a relatively new resident may develop the inspiration to begin a community building initiative, then fail miserably because he or she did not adequately understand the community culture. Conversely, a nonresident of a community who has had a relationship with the community over a long period of time may have an excellent understanding upon which to start a community building initiative.[24]

Questions for Community Builders

- Do the organizers for this community building effort understand how decisions are made in the community?

- Do the organizers for this community building effort understand the social norms, values, and culture of the community?

- Do the organizers of this community building effort understand the history of the community?

- Do the organizers of this community building effort understand the demographic make-up of different groups in the community and how they relate to one another?

- Do organizers of this effort understand the needs, frustrations, and problems facing the community?

3B. Sincerity of Commitment

Successful community building efforts are more likely to occur when organized by individuals who convey a sincere commitment to the community's well-being. Community residents must perceive these individuals as:

- Interested in the community's long-term well-being

- Having a sustained attachment to community members (at least during the initiative)

- Honest

- Acting primarily to serve the interests of the community, not of an external group.

A study that looked at characteristics of successful leaders in a number of community building efforts in India determined that "effective leaders were generally those who were respected and accepted because they showed desire to improve the communities rather than gain what personal status might accrue from leadership activities." (Clinard, 1970:260)

---

[24] Rivera and Erlich (1992) refer to "levels of intimacy" and offer examples of individuals who reside in a community and have good intentions to promote social capacity, but who lack the necessary intimacy with cultural norms, social networks, and so forth.

Questions for Community Builders

- Do the organizers for this community building effort have the best interest of the community in mind?

- Do community members believe the organizers are fair?

- Do the organizers spend time in the community getting to know people?

- Do the organizers plan to be involved over a long period of time?

- Do the organizers stay with the effort even through the hard times to help the community overcome obstacles?

3C. A Relationship of Trust

Successful efforts are more likely to occur when the organizers develop trusting relationships with community residents. Trust is an essential element of all human relationships, so little surprise should result from the documentation by research of its importance for community building. Community building often requires risk taking, arduous task accomplishment, great patience and endurance over long periods of time, and other activities which consume time and energy. The work can be physically and emotionally draining.[25] Community members need to rely upon one another in such a way that they all know:

- They and the community organizer share a common mission or vision. The major reason for participating in the community building initiative is similar across participants.

- The community organizer is looking out for their best interests and will not be exploitive.

- The community organizer does not favor one group over another.

- They and the community organizer have a common vocabulary. When they communicate with one another, all parties have the same understanding.

- The community organizer will follow through on his or her commitments.

An example from southern Appalachia illustrates the importance of local acceptance:

> A community organizer affiliated with a local university was asked to help with a community that was in desperate economic shape facing an uncertain future. Before even entering

---

[25] In extreme situations, of course, it can literally be life threatening, as when community building efforts challenge the control and threaten the power base of individuals with a propensity for violence.

the community the organizer wrote letters to the local missionary, who had invited him, to help clarify the local problems. At his first visit the organizer and his wife spent most of the time talking with the local residents. Prior to visiting the homes of these local people, they asked the local missionary, who knew the local people well, to circulate word that the visitors were kindly folk who were to be trusted.

The organizer and his wife were welcomed into the community and were able to talk with many community members during their visit. (Biddle and Biddle, 1965:11)

In another example, the community organizer had to prove to the community that he was there for all members of the community—not just to serve the interests of one group.

The consultant lived most of each week in the local hotel. He spent day and night talking to organizations, clubs, church congregations (which included sermons from the pulpit), informal gatherings; he accepted invitations to family dinners and talked with people in their homes, reaching into all levels of the local class structure, all the while talking about the importance of everyone being involved and having faith in working out the future of the community together. A good portion of the work during these weeks was to steer off any identification of the program with any one particular group in town. . . . The consultant established very close personal relationships with people in all levels of the community, and gradually the program did come to be regarded as an activity which included all Eldorado. (Bruyn, 1963:57)

Questions for Community Builders

- Has the organizer spent time developing relationships with people in the community?

- Does the person organizing this community building initiative have the skills to build trusting relationships with community members?

- Does the community organizer favor some community members over others? [26]

- Does the community organizer have the same goals and mission as the rest of the community members?

- Do community members trust that the organizer will follow through on commitments?

[26] Delgado (1993) raises this issue in his article.

3D. Level of Organizing Experience

Successful community building efforts are more likely when the organizers are experienced. Other things being equal, organizers with longer experience and with a wider breadth of experience bring the community building effort to fruition more effectively than inexperienced organizers.

Advantages that an experienced community building organizer brings to an initiative include:

- Ability to realistically appraise requirements for completing work
- Ability to work with and motivate people
- Ability to plan activities and to be productive

A study of community building as part of a broader community development demonstration program undertaken by the Local Initiatives Support Corporation (LISC) provides an example of how a skilled organizer can make a difference in the community building process—in this case, by having the ability to assess leadership potential among community residents:

> In Boynton Beach, the organizer recognized a strong potential leader in Art Mathews, an African American businessman who owned a store in the neighborhood and who saw the CDC as a unique opportunity to make things change there. The organizer helped point out his potential to other volunteers, and encouraged Mathews himself to seriously consider taking on the job. He did. The other volunteers responded to his enthusiasm, his willingness to take charge, and his even-handed approach to leading the group. (Gittel, Vidal, and Turner, 1994:20)

Questions for Community Builders

- What type of experience do we want a community organizer to have?
- Do community organizer candidates for this effort have the experience needed?
- Is there training or technical assistance available to fill in the gaps in the organizer's experience?

3E. Able to be Flexible and Adaptable

Successful community building efforts are more likely when organizers are flexible and able to adapt to constantly changing situations and environments. Community building efforts that have been around a long time have gone through many changes organizationally, functionally, and in regard to the people involved.

Meredith Minkler discusses the continuous evolution of models for organizing that were employed at different times over the fifteen years the Tenderloin Senior Organizing Project was in operation. In the beginning, the organizing was much more service oriented (providing breakfast programs and staffing food co-ops), while in later years the organizers were less service oriented and provided more leadership training and technical assistance. The changes were the result of observation and learning by project organizers who were able to respond to new information to find better ways of building social capacity.

In some cases, organizers are members of government bureaucracies that would like increased local participation in decision making. Korten (1980) found that organizers from government programs often hindered the community building process because of inflexible rules, agendas, and their inability to adapt to the needs of the communities they were working with.

Questions for Community Builders

- Are the organizers able to adapt to changing situations, people, politics, and social climates?
- Are the organizers and the organizations they represent flexible in their approach and able to adapt to the needs of the community?

The Need for Future Research

The factors identified in this research need to be confirmed and quantified. We hope that researchers interested in community building develop good measures of these factors, and that they conduct additional studies to add more precision and depth to our understanding of what makes community building successful.

Better research would tell us such things as:

- Are some factors more important than others?
- How do these factors relate to one another?
- Are some factors more important in certain types of communities?
- Is it more difficult to achieve certain factors in certain types of communities?

Answering such questions would provide useful information to those in the field attempting to do significant work improving communities.

Chapter Four
Suggestions for Using This Material

Community building might be likened to improving physical capacity. If this book were about running, we would identify the factors that lead to success at running—the factors that enable us to increase our capacity to run farther, run longer, win the next 5K race, or run a marathon. Chapters Two and Three would identify these factors, such as nutrition, practice routines, or attributes of coaches. In consulting these chapters, with the goal of improving our performance, we would notice several things:

- The factors only improve our *capacity*. Increasing the level to which we have them does not guarantee that we will win a race, only that we will have a much better chance of doing so.

  Similarly, the factors that lead to successful community building only increase community social capacity. They put a community in much better condition to accomplish tasks and resolve problems, but they do not guarantee that a community will accomplish everything it wants to accomplish.

- We will already have greater or lesser amounts of each factor, and this will influence how, and how quickly, we can make progress.

  Similarly, different communities will have different levels of social capacity at the time they initiate community building efforts. Those with more social capacity may progress much more quickly, and members of such communities can set their expectations accordingly.

- The precise mix of factors will differ from individual to individual, depending upon the ultimate goals they want to achieve, their existing level of capacity, and the environment in which they find themselves.

  Similarly, every community that initiates a community building effort will need to assess itself to determine which, if any, factors need work in order to make a community building effort successful.

Using the Information

We know that the readers of this report include a wide range of individuals with an interest in community building:

- Individuals who want to improve the quality of life in the place where they live.

- Nonprofit and government agency managers and staff whose work includes participation in, or support of, community building initiatives.

- Professional community organizers and developers who work with, or advise, groups interested in community building.

- Funders, policy makers, and other decision makers who need to allocate resources based on the most cost-efficient means to reach significant social goals—and who want to make sure that, if they fund an effort, it has the greatest chance of success.

- Others who take part in any way in community building activities.

We hope our work provides a theoretical understanding of the elements of successful community building efforts. We believe you will find it a sound overview of what makes community building successful, but you still need to decide on your own how to apply that knowledge.

For example, the research clearly indicates the importance of good communication. However, a variety of ways exist to promote and accomplish good communication. The best approach will vary from situation to situation.

Further, you must temper the factors we've uncovered with your own experience. Because of the nature of this research, it's possible other factors exist that weren't identified.

Use This Information for General Understanding . . .

One use of the report is for general understanding. Read it to increase your knowledge of the success factors behind community building efforts. You will then have a set of useful concepts in mind when you plan any community building work.

Some questions you might raise when considering a community building effort:

- Will it be possible, as best as you can estimate, to include all the factors necessary for success in your situation?

- What will be the cost (time, money, other resources) of doing whatever it takes to make sure the success factors are included? Do the expected benefits of the community building effort exceed the potential costs?

Use This Information in Specific Situations . . .

Once you have decided to proceed with an effort, or if you are in the middle of an effort, you might want to turn to this report when you need to formulate specific plans or make a decision. The materials in Chapters Two and Three can serve you in at least three ways:

1. Use the set of success factors as a checklist to determine if your group's plans include all necessary components. If not, you can take steps to build in whatever the project lacks.

   Questions you might want to ask include:

   - How does a proposed effort rate on each of the factors? For example, is there community awareness of a problem (Factor 1A)? Does motivation exist within the community (Factor 1B)?

   - If a proposed project rates low on a specific factor, is that a reason not to proceed or can steps be taken to improve this rating?

   - Has the planning for an effort built in mechanisms for both *developing* and *sustaining* the factors necessary for success?

2. Use the content of Chapters Two and Three to expand your thinking about ways to help your community building effort to succeed, comparing your situation with others that might be similar.

   For example, successful efforts are more likely to occur when participants receive training to gain community building skills (group facilitation, gathering assessment information, understanding the political process). What techniques will your group use—mentoring, community workshops, or some other method?

3. After you have a community building effort under way, return to the material in the report to ask: What should we be watching out for? Are there changes we need to make in mid-course?

   For example, you might find that you and other members of the community have spent much time making sure there is widespread participation (Factor 2A) in the community building effort. However, a period of time has passed, and no new members of the community have come into the effort. Is the continuous effort to recruit new members lacking? Are existing members burning out? Is the group stagnating?

Community building is not a one-time event. Efforts take place over months, years, even decades. The individual factors we have identified overlap; they may come into play at different times in the process, may be of little value in certain activities and absolutely critical to others. No doubt, factors other than those we've identified through the literature also come into play. In the end, community building is an art—not a science. We hope that the work we've done in analyzing and synthesizing the literature will give you new tools and new vocabulary to think what works, as well as what doesn't work.

Definitions

A

During our research, we uncovered many terms and words used by people working to improve communities. Many of those terms had different meanings to different people. This presents a problem for both researchers and practitioners in the field.

Developing consensus about a solution to community problems is difficult enough. Add in the vagueness of common terms to describe different aspects of the process, and the task is almost insurmountable. Advocates have a difficult time presenting a united front to policy makers, service providers, and funders when common terms for describing their work are used in different ways. In addition, the ambiguity of terms and language contributes to misunderstandings between funders and recipients. Vague terminology makes it difficult for practitioners to clearly communicate with clients and colleagues. Researchers don't have common terms to develop a comparable body of literature that will advance the field.

Agreement and understanding about common terms may help us all communicate more clearly as we work to increase community and neighborhood capacity to solve problems.

Our goal in this appendix is to identify common terms, provide the definitions developed by different authors, describe some of the different ways these terms are used, and explain our choice of definitions.

Here are some terms we uncovered in our literature search:

- Community
- Community Development
- Community Organizing
- Community Building
- Capacity Building
- Social Capital
- Community Competence
- Empowerment

Community

The term *community* can include the dimensions of geographic location, psychological ties, and/or people working together toward a common goal.

We chose to use the following definition:

> *People who live within a geographically defined area and who have social and psychological ties with each other and with the place where they live.*

We adopted this definition because it focuses attention on communities which most people would characterize as "residential." It can easily include urban neighborhoods, small towns, or other areas which people identify as the "place where they live." Other types of communities certainly have great importance. However, we wanted to limit our focus to residential communities. And, indeed, most social research studies focus on this type of community.

Examples of definitions of community

We found many definitions of "community." Here are a few of them.

> Community is "a grouping of people who live close to one another and are united by common interests and mutual aid." (The National Research Council, 1975)

> Community is "people that live within a geographically bounded area who are involved in social interaction and have one or more psychological ties with each other and with the place in which they live." (Christenson and Robinson, 1989)

"Community is whatever sense of the local common good citizens can be helped to achieve. This perception of community is an achievement, not something given by reason of geographic residence. It is not fixed; it changes as a result of experience or purposeful effort. It may even shift according to the problem that catches the attention of the citizens." (Biddle and Biddle, 1965)

Community is "that combination of social units and systems which perform the major social functions having locality relevance. The organization of social activities to afford people daily local access to those broad areas of activity which are necessary in day-to-day living." (Warren, 1963)

"Community is a feeling that members have of belonging, a feeling that members matter to one another and to the group, and a shared faith that members' needs will be met through their commitment to be together." (McMillan and Chavis, 1986)

Community Development

Community development definitions tend to share the common elements of a process of bringing people together to achieve a common goal, usually related to changing the quality of life. Some definitions involve the process of building networks and improving the capacity of individuals and organizations. Here is one such example: [Community development is] "An educational approach which would raise levels of local awareness and increase the confidence and ability of community groups to identify and tackle their own problems." (Darby and Morris, 1975, in Christenson and Robinson, 1989.)

Other definitions focus more on improvements within the community without necessarily working on relationship building. As an example: [Community development is] "A group of people in a locality initiating a social action process (i.e., planned intervention) to change their economic, social, cultural, and/or environmental situation." (Christenson and Robinson, 1989). In this definition, the purpose of community development is to improve the economic, social, cultural, or environmental well-being. Within this definition, it would be acceptable to make such improvements without increasing community members' skills, networks, or relationships.

Our research review focuses mostly on community building, which can be one aspect of community development. So as not to confuse our readers, we have purposely avoided the term *community development* because it implies an ultimate change in some quality of life indicator such as increased economic opportunities, more housing, or improved health, without necessarily improving the community's ability to solve problems collectively. If we were to measure the outcomes in a community development project, the measures might include reduction in homelessness or reduced infant mortality. If we were to measure the outcomes in community building, we might look at whether the process strengthened community ties, whether community members came to consensus about how to solve a problem, or whether they worked collaboratively to solve a problem.

Examples of definitions of community development

"Community development is a social process by which human beings can become more competent to live with and gain some control over local aspects of a frustrating and changing world." (Biddle and Biddle, 1965)

Community development "aims to educate and motivate people for self-help; to develop responsible local leadership; to inculcate among the members of rural communities a sense of citizenship and among the residents of urban areas a spirit of civic consciousness; to introduce and strengthen democracy at the grass-roots level through the creation and/or revitalization of institutions designed to serve as instruments of local participation; to initiate a self-generative, self-sustaining, and enduring process of growth; to enable people to establish and maintain cooperative and harmonious relationships; and to bring about gradual and self-chosen changes in the community's life with a minimum of stress and disruption." (Khinduka, in Cox et al., 1979)

Community development is "a deliberate, democratic, developmental activity; focusing on an existing social and geographical grouping of people; who participate in the solution of common problems for the common good." (Cawley, 1984, in Christenson and Robinson, 1989)

Community development is "the process of local decision making and the development of programs designed to make [the] community a better place to live and work." (Huie, 1976, in Christenson and Robinson, 1989)

Community development is "an educational process designed to help adults in a community solve their problems by group decision making and group action. Most community development models include broad citizen involvement and training in problem solving." (Long, 1975, in Christenson and Robinson, 1989)

Community development is "a process in which increasingly more members of a given area or environment make and implement socially responsible decisions, the probable consequence of which is an increase in the life chances of some people without a decrease in the life chances of others." (Oberle, Darby, and Stowers, 1975, in Christenson and Robinson, 1989)

Community development is "the active voluntary involvement in a process to improve some identifiable aspect of community life; normally such action leads to the strengthening of the community's pattern of human and institutional interrelationships." (Ploch, 1976, in Christenson and Robinson, 1989)

Community development is "the active involvement of people at the level of the local community in resisting or supporting some cause or issue or program that interests them." (Ravitz, 1982, in Christenson and Robinson, 1989)

Community development is "a situation in which some groups, usually locality-based such as a neighborhood or local community . . . attempt to improve [their] social and economic situation through [their] own efforts . . . using professional assistance and perhaps also financial assistance from the outside . . . and involving all sectors of the community or group to a maximum." (Voth, 1975, in Christenson and Robinson, 1989)

Community development is "acts by people that open and maintain channels of communication and cooperation among local groups." (Wilkinson, 1979, in Christenson and Robinson, 1989)

Community development is "the process by which the efforts of the people themselves are united with those of governmental authorities to improve the economic, social, and cultural conditions of communities, to integrate these communities into the life of the nation, and to enable them to contribute fully to national progress. This complex of processes is, therefore, made up of two essential elements: the participation by the people themselves in efforts to improve their level of living, with as much reliance as possible on their own initiative; and the provision of technical and other services in ways which encourage initiative, self-help and mutual help and make these more effective. It is expressed in programs designed to achieve a wide variety of specific improvements." (The United Nations, 1963, in Christenson and Robinson, 1989)

Community development is "a series of community improvements which take place over time as a result of the common efforts of various groups of people. Each successive improvement is a discrete unit of community development. It meets a human want or need." (Dunbar, 1972, in Christenson and Robinson, 1989)

Community development is "an orchestrated attempt to influence a person or a system in relation to some goal which an actor desires." (Tropman and Erlich, in Cox et al., 1979)

Community Organizing

Community organizing refers to the process of bringing community members together and providing them with the tools to help themselves. Community organizing is a strategy for building communities and for community development.

Here is a useful definition we found in the recent literature.

> We conceive of community organizing as a long-term, relationship-building and capacity-building process that attempts to identify, include, and build upon a range of key resources, both internal and external to the community. . . . The process includes: the identification of key local resources, the gathering of information about the community context, the development and training of local leaders to prepare them to serve effectively as representatives of the community and as full partners in an initiative, and the strengthening of the network of the various interests both internal and external to a community. (Joseph and Ogletree, 1996)

Community Building

Community building generally refers to building the social networks within the community, and developing group and individual problem-solving and leadership skills. Our definition of community building is:

> *Any identifiable set of activities pursued by a community in order to increase community social capacity*

Examples of definitions of community building

> "Community building is an ongoing comprehensive effort that strengthens the norms, supports, and problem-solving resources of the community." (Committee for Economic Development, 1995)

> Community building is "the practice of building connections among residents, and establishing positive patterns of individual and community behavior based on mutual responsibility and ownership." (Gardner in Leiterman, 1993, p.6)

> "Fundamentally, community building concerns strengthening the capacity of neighborhood residents, associations, and organizations to work, individually and collectively to foster and sustain positive neighborhood change. For individuals, community building focuses on both the capacity and 'empowerment' of neighborhood residents to identify and access opportunities and effect change, as well as on

the development of individual leadership. For associations, community building focuses on the nature, strength, and scope of relationships (both affective and instrumental) among individuals within the neighborhood and through them, connections to networks of association beyond the neighborhood. These are ties through kinship, acquaintance or other more formal means through which information, resources, and assistance can be received and delivered. Finally, for organizations, community building centers on developing the capacity of formal and informal institutions within the neighborhood to provide goods and services effectively, and on the relationships among organizations both within and beyond the neighborhood to maximize resources and coordinate strategies." (Kubisch et al., 1995)

Capacity Building and Our Definition of Social Capacity

The definitions of capacity can include any one or all of the following elements: the commitment and motivation a community has, the ability to organize and utilize resources, the ability to understand and analyze problems, and the skills to solve problems together. Some people have also used this term to refer to the abilities of community agencies and institutions as well as individuals.

Our work in this report concerns the capacity of individuals to work together. We felt this was a useful definition but did not include a strong enough emphasis on the social support aspect of community building. We added *social* to *capacity* to increase the focus on social networks. Our definition of social capacity is:

> *The extent to which members of a community can work together effectively.*

This definition includes the abilities to:

- Develop and sustain strong relationships
- Solve problems and make group decisions
- Collaborate effectively to identify goals and get work done

When we refer to capacity building, we mean the building of social capacity.

Examples of definitions of capacity building

> Capacity building is "the abilities of residents to organize and mobilize their resources for the accomplishment of consensual defined goals." (Christenson and Robinson, 1989)

"Community capacity is the combined influence of a community's commitment, resources, and skills which can be deployed to build on community strengths and address community problems." (Mayer, Rainbow Research, 1994)

"Capacity is being able to successfully cope with problems of increasing variety and complexity." (Rubin and Rubin, 1986)

"Capacity building . . . describes activity to enhance leadership skills, group problem solving, collaborative methods, and substantive understanding of community assets, problems and opportunities among organized, participating community residents." (McNeely, 1996:87)

Social Capital

Social capital refers to the resources such as skills, knowledge, reciprocity, and norms and values that make it easier for people to work together. Our definition of social capacity is similar to the definition of social capital. However, we chose to use the term social capacity because we found that more practitioners used it.

A definition of social capital

Social capital is "the resources embedded in social relations among persons and organizations that facilitate cooperation and collaboration in communities. Like physical and human capital, social capital is a productive resource that makes possible otherwise unachievable results and enhances the productivity of other resources. For example, educated parents (human capital) benefit their child if parents and child spend time interacting (social capital). . . . Social capital exists in three principal forms: First, information sharing uses social relations to convey valuable information. Thus, a parent seeking child care may consult friends, relatives, or neighbors who have experience with local child care providers. Second, trust engendered through social relations establishes generalized reciprocity as a norm within a community: 'I'll do this for you now because you (or someone else) will assist me later.' This process does not require specific reciprocation; rather, it is a shared expectation that if residents need help, they will receive it. Third, norms and values that maintain social order—social expectations such as delaying childbearing until marriage or investing in education—are passed on in families, schools, churches, and other settings. They are reinforced by social support, honors, and rewards, whereas failure to comply with expectations is sanctioned by punishment or loss of status." (Committee for Economic Development, 1995)

Community Competence

The term *community competence* was developed by Leonard Cottrell as a way to define how a well-functioning community behaves. We liked the specificity and measurability of this term, as well as the fact that it had been used in other research. However, the term *competence* has some negative connotations. For example, if a community lacks certain abilities, are they incompetent (a truly loaded word)? To put a more positive spin on the concept we decided to use some of the ideas of community competence and include them in the term *community social capacity*.

Leonard Cotrell developed this definition of a competent community:

"A Competent Community is one in which its various parts are able to:

1. Collaborate effectively in identifying the problems and needs of a community

2. Achieve a workable consensus on goals and priorities.

3. Agree on ways and means to implement the agreed-upon goal.

4. Collaborate effectively in the required activity." (Cottrell, 1976)

Empowerment

Empowerment has a broad range of meanings in the literature. The term can be legalistic, such as in granting official or legal powers, or it can refer to the concept of people participating in decisions about matters that will affect them, or it can refer to enabling something to happen, or even to personal self-actualization.

The Cornell Empowerment Project definition comes close to our definition of community building. While empowerment is used by some people in community building, we feel *community building* is a more specific term than empowerment and less likely to be misinterpreted because it doesn't have as many different connotations.

Examples of definitions of empowerment

Empowerment is "to give official authority or legal power to. . . . To promote the self-actualization or influence of." (Merriam-Webster's Collegiate Dictionary, Tenth Edition, 1993)

"Empowerment is obtained by building individual capacity through mobilizing resources." (Rubin and Rubin, 1986)

"Empowerment is the intentional ongoing process, centered in the local community, involving mutual respect, critical reflection, caring and group participation through which people lacking in a proportional share of the resources gain greater access to and control over those resources." (Cornell Empowerment Project, 1989)

Appendix B
Methodology

Once we decided on the general research question, we dove into the work of reviewing, analyzing, and synthesizing the literature. Just as a detective needs to systematically collect clues in a criminal investigation, we needed to have a systematic process for collecting information about what works to build communities.

We did this work in three stages. First, we identified and assessed research studies related to our topic. Second, as we developed our list of relevant studies, we started to systematically codify the findings of each study. Third, we then synthesized the findings of the individual studies into categories. This process took about a-year-and-a-half to complete, with two staff people working part-time. We tried to document each part of the process so that if other researchers want to replicate this study, they can do so.

Identification and Assessment of Research Studies

A. Formulation of a Precise Research Question

After an initial review of some of the literature, we formulated a precise research question. This question provided a guide for our complete review of the literature:

> *What factors influence the success of community building efforts? That is, what factors influence the success of activities carried out in an effort to increase community social capacity?*

This question oriented the work in several ways. It established that the research to be included in the review must:

- Focus on community building.

- Relate to the success of a community building effort (measured in terms of outcomes)—not merely to the reasons for trying to strengthen communities, or to process alone without outcomes. For example, the author must describe the community members as having developed better skills at building consensus, or must show that the community was more cohesive as a result of the community building effort.

B. Collection of Potentially Relevant Studies

Our staff searched for and collected any studies which seemed to relate to the principal research question. We followed two major routes: (1) identification of research through computer database searches; and (2) contacts with experts in the field.

Identification of research through computer database searches

We searched the following computerized databases for appropriate studies: Psychological Abstracts, Sociological Abstracts, Public Affairs Information Service, Medline, and the Educational Resources Information Center. Key words and terms used in our search included the following:

- community development
- community organizing
- capacity building
- neighborhood development
- grassroots development
- grassroots organizing
- community empowerment
- community change
- community participation
- international community development
- sustainable development
- successful development

We also used other on-line services such as the Internet and HandsNet, a subscription on-line service for human service professionals.

Identification of research through contacting experts in the field

We talked with over thirty experts working in both academic and community settings, as well as representatives of clearinghouses and resource centers, to obtain suggestions of available studies. The complete contact list appears in Appendix C.

We asked, "Are you aware of any evaluations or research case studies of community building projects we could use for our study?" Based on their responses, we tracked down specific studies, or made additional contacts.

Our research staff identified additional sources through bibliographies and citations. All materials were documented and entered into a computer database for tracking. The search for new studies could, of course, continue indefinitely, since new research appears everyday. However, we pursued new sources aggressively until we reached the point where the yield from new contacts or new bibliographies began to overlap almost completely with our existing database.

After eighteen months, we finally compiled a list of 525 studies to be assessed as to whether they would be included in the review.

Assessment to determine which studies to include

Collecting the studies was just a start. We needed to sift through them to uncover those that would help us understand community building and answer our basic research question. (What factors influence the success of community building efforts? That is, what factors influence the success of activities carried out in an effort to increase social capacity?)

To decide which studies had adequate value to be part of the review, we developed a set of criteria. If a study satisfied all the criteria, it remained in the review.

1. The study must address the major research question (as described above).

2. The study must include a measure of success. The measure must reflect some sort of empirical observations.[27]

3. The research method used by the author must be at least a careful case study analysis, if not a more rigorous method, such as an experimental design with control groups, statistical tests, and valid, reliable collection of quantitative data.

---

[27] Note, however, that the measure of success need not appear explicitly in the text of a study report. It could be stated, for example, in bits and pieces, in various portions of the report—so long as the research team could figure out what measurement method was used.

4. The study must have sufficient documentation of its research method to determine that the observations or data collection relate to the conclusions.

5. Projects providing the data for the study must have occurred after 1950.

6. The study findings must appear in a written document, including government reports, conference papers, unpublished manuscripts, masters theses, dissertations, journal articles, and books.

7. The study could be national or international, in any type of setting (urban, rural, international).

8. The study must be available in English. It could be written in another language originally, but must already have been translated.

In addition, if the research was a case study, the work must include:

- A complete explanation of development activities being studied

- Enough data collected to provide evidence in support of the author's conclusions

- Evidence that appears unbiased

- Explicit links between the questions asked, the data collected, and the conclusions drawn

Studies meeting these criteria were retained in the review. This screening reduced the number of studies to forty-eight.

The most significant difficulty in this stage of the research review was that despite the existence of published material on our topic, very little of this material comes in the form of carefully designed research studies. Thus, our method required many hours of sifting through materials, and sometimes multiple readings of articles by multiple readers to decide if the study met our criteria. In the end, we felt confident that the final group of studies selected were methodologically strong and applied to our research question.

Systematic Codification of Findings from Each Individual Study

A. Establishing Rules for Identifying Factors

Research on community building typically involves case studies. This increases the difficulty of pooling findings of multiple studies because they do not contain quantitative data, with similar definitions. Therefore, we needed to develop a way to:

- Identify the success factors that each case study demonstrated.
- Indicate the weight or importance or each factor as an influence on success so we could determine whether, in the final analysis, to retain a specific factor.

The primary rules we developed for culling success factors from case studies were that:

1. The case study must include a statement by the case researcher that a particular factor influenced the success of the community building effort that was studied.

2. It must be possible for the reader of a study (in this case, research staff) to link the statement by the case researcher about the factor directly to evidence in the case study about its effect upon success. For example, if an author describes leadership training as a factor that influenced success in a community building effort, then there must be evidence that community members attended leadership training, and that the training increased their ability to perform tasks related to community building, such as facilitating meetings or planning events.

Even within a review of empirical research studies, this can be a difficult task. When working with case studies, it becomes a monumental challenge.

B. Identification of Factors

A member of the research team carefully reviewed each study, identifying factors that were stated in the study to influence success and which could be linked to evidence in the study.

C. Validation of Factors

A second member of the research team independently reviewed the case studies and the work of the first researcher to make sure each factor met the two criteria listed in item (A) above.

Synthesis of Findings from Individual Studies

A. Determining an Initial, Draft List of Factors

As we uncovered the factors, we listed them on a worksheet, including their source and its author. Two researchers independently reviewed each factor on the list to determine whether certain factors were the same and could eventually be collapsed into one. In some cases, the wording of factors in two or more studies was identical, and they could easily be counted as the same. In other cases, the wording differed, and research staff had to decide whether different authors were using different terms to refer to the same concept.

B. Eliminating the Factors with the Weakest Evidence

Case studies, as noted earlier, make it difficult to assess the relative importance, or weight, of each factor. Therefore, the research team developed a procedure to eliminate factors that seemed to have the weakest evidence. We did this to increase the probability that the list will not contain a factor which is not well substantiated by the research evidence.

Recall that all the studies still included at this point met, at least, our eight criteria, and that all of the factors met our two criteria for factors. In this last round of screening, we eliminated all factors that could not meet at least one of the following tests:

- Identification by at least four authors of single or double community studies.

- Identification by at least one author of a multiple (three or more) community study.

At this point, twenty-eight factors remained.

C. Putting the Factors into Categories

For ease of presentation, discussion, and use, we grouped the factors into three categories: Characteristics of the Community, Characteristics of the Community Building Process, and Characteristics of Community Building Organizers. This placement makes intuitive sense to us. However, readers can regroup the factors into different categories without compromising the work of this report.

Appendix C
Community Building Resources and Contacts

This is a list of resources we contacted for our literature search. Many have research and informational literature available.

There are many agencies and individuals in both the public and private sector that provide resources in community development and community building. (An Internet search pulled up over 400,000 hits using the term community development.) The list that follows is not meant to be a complete list of resources. It consists of the organizations we contacted. If you are interested in learning more about community building, we believe any of these organizations would be a good place to start looking.

The Applied Research Center
25 Embarcadero Cove
Oakland, CA 94606

The Applied Research Center (ARC), through a framework derived from community organizing, seeks to develop critical analyses, forge collaborative initiatives, and build strategic support for progressive social change. They have a publications list and newsletters available.

CARE
660 First Avenue
New York, NY 10016

CARE is an international development organization.

Center for Community Change
100 Wisconsin Avenue Northwest
Washington, DC 20007

The Center for Community Change provides training to help grassroots leaders build strong community-based organizations. The Center provides a variety of assistance to organizations that work in low-income communities, helping them get started, develop effective boards, raise money, organize their communities, set objectives, devise strategies, build housing, and develop a stronger local economy. They have a publications list and newsletter.

Center for Integrated Services for Families and Neighborhoods
1620 Sixth Street
Sacramento, CA 95814

The Center for Integrated Services for Families and Neighborhoods was founded in February 1992, with a mission of reforming the human service system by offering technical assistance and guidance to system change efforts. It has been working with local leaders in several low-income, distressed communities to establish integrated neighborhood service systems. *Editor's note: The Center for Integrated Services for Families and Neighborhoods closed during the final stages of this research project.*

Center for Neighborhood Technology
2125 West North Avenue
Chicago, IL 60647

Founded in 1978, the Center for Neighborhood Technology seeks affordable, appropriately scaled, locally controlled ways for city residents to meet basic needs for food, housing, jobs, and a healthy environment. They work with low- and moderate-income neighborhoods in Chicago and other urban settings. They have a newsletter and other publications for neighborhood groups working on a variety of issues.

Chapin Hall Center for Children
The University of Chicago
1155 East Sixtieth Street
Chicago, IL 60637

Chapin Hall Center for Children at the University of Chicago is an independent research and development center dedicated to the study of issues affecting children. They evaluate and study community building initiatives as they relate to child and family well-being. Publications list available.

Community Development Foundation
60 Highbury Grove
London N5 2AG

Tel: 0171 226 5375

The Community Development Foundation (CDF) was set up in 1968 to pioneer new forms of community development. CDF strengthens communities by ensuring the effective participation of people in determining the conditions that affect their lives. It does this through providing support for community initiatives, promoting best practice, and informing policy makers at the local and national level. Their focus of interest is the United Kingdom and Europe. They have a publications list and newsletter.

Community Development Research Center
New School for Social Research
Graduate School of Management and Urban Policy
66 Fifth Avenue
Room 812
New York, NY 10011

(212) 229-5415

This is an academic research center at the New School for Social Research. They have a publications list.

The Community Information Exchange
1029 Vermont Avenue Northwest
Suite 710
Washington, DC 20005

(202) 628-2981

The Community Information Exchange is a nonprofit information and technical assistance provider. The Exchange manages a database of research, case examples, and technical assistance providers. They also have newsletters and research briefs available.

Direct Action and Research Training Center (DART)
137 Northeast Nineteenth Street
Miami, FL 33132

DART provides training and consultation on community organizing.

Gamaliel Foundation
220 South State Street
Chicago, IL 60604

Gamaliel Foundation is a leadership training organization.

Highlander Research and Education Center
1959 Highlander Way
New Market, TN 37820

Highlander provides leadership training programs. They have a publications list.

Institute for Social Justice Association of Community Organizations for Reform Now (ACORN)
523 West Fifteenth Street
Little Rock, AR 72202

Training organization for members of ACORN.

Kentuckians for the Commonwealth
425 West Mohammed Ali Boulevard
Suite 328
Louisville, KY 40202

This organization provides training on community organizing.

Local Initiatives Support Corporation (LISC)
733 Third Avenue
New York, NY 10017

(212) 455-9800

Created in 1979, LISC is the nation's largest national nonprofit community development intermediary, channeling private investment from corporations and foundations as loans and equity supporting the efforts of community development corporations to rebuild inner-city neighborhoods.

Midwest Academy
225 West Ohio Street
Suite 250
Chicago, IL 60610

The Midwest Academy provides training on community organizing. Their publication, *Organizing for Social Change: A Manual for Activists in the 1990s,* by Kim Bobo, Jackie Kendall, and Steve Max, is a resource for organizers and includes many support organizations.

The National Community Building Network
Urban Strategies Council
672 Thirteenth Street
Suite 200
Oakland, CA 94612

(510) 893-2404

The National Community Building Network focuses on two primary goals: (1) Influencing public policy on urban affairs, especially national policy; and (2) Providing a forum for urban community planners and activists to learn from each other and exchange ideas.

National Organizers Alliance
130 West Eleventh Street Northeast
Washington, DC 20002

National Organizers Alliance is a professional organization for community organizers.

National Housing Institute
439 Main Street
Orange, NJ 07050

Provides training for tenant and community groups. Publishes a newsletter.

OxFam America
115 Broadway
Boston, MA 02116

This is an international development organization.

Partners for Livable Communities
1429 Twenty-first Street Northwest
Washington, DC 20036

Partners for Livable Communities is a nonprofit organization working to improve the livability of communities by promoting quality of life, economic development, and social equity. Founded in 1977, Partners helps communities set common visions for the future, discover and use new resources for community and economic development, and build public/private coalitions to further their goals. A publications list and newsletter are available.

Peace Corps
1990 K Street Northwest
Washington, DC 20526

This is an international development organization that provides training to volunteers.

Rainbow Research, Inc.
621 West Lake Street
Minneapolis, MN 55408

(612) 824-0724

Rainbow Research provides research, evaluation, and technical assistance services to socially concerned organizations and community groups. They have a publications list.

Search Institute
700 South Third Street
Suite 210
Minneapolis, MN 55415

Search Institute is an independent research and educational organization working to advance the well-being and positive development of children and adolescents through applied research, evaluation, consultation, training, and the development of publications and practical resources.

Southern Empowerment Project (SEP)
323 Ellis Avenue
Maryville, TN 37801

This organization provides leadership training.

Wilder Research Center
1295 Bandana Boulevard North
Suite 210
Saint Paul, MN 55108

Wilder Research Center's mission is to strengthen individuals, families, and communities through research. Their forty-plus research staff conduct evaluation research, trend studies, and policy studies related to communities.

Individuals Contacted

The following is a list of individuals who were contacted for advice about this research project.

Renee Berger, Teamworks, San Francisco, CA

Arthur Bolton, Center for Integrated Services for Families and Neighborhoods, Sacramento, CA

Harry Boyte, University of Minnesota, Minneapolis, MN

Eric Brettschneider, Agenda For Children Tomorrow, New York City

Prudence Brown, Chapin Hall Center for Children, University of Chicago, Chicago, IL

John Calkins, Direct Action Research and Training Center (DART), Miami, FL

Robert Chaskin, Chapin Hall Center for Children, University of Chicago, Chicago, IL

Gale Cincotta, National Training and Information Center of National People's Action, Chicago, IL

Pat Costigan, The Enterprise Foundation, Baltimore, MD

Walter Davis, Southern Empowerment Project, Maryville, TN

Lisa Donaldson, The Atlanta Project, Atlanta, GA

Michael Eichler, Consensus Organizing Institute, Boston, MA

Kim Fellner, National Organizers Alliance, Washington, DC

Robert Fisher, University of Houston, Houston, TX

Gregory Galluzzo, Gamaliel Foundation, Chicago, IL

Rober Giloth, Annie B. Casey Foundation, Baltimore, MD

Susan Goetz, The Applied Research Center, Oakland, CA

Jordon Hamoway, Comprehensive Community Revitalization Program, Surdna Foundation, New York City

Ann Kubisch, The Aspen Institute, Washington, DC

Mindy Leiterman, Local Initiative Support Corporation, New York City

John McKnight, Northwestern University, Evanston, IL

Meredith Minkler, School of Public Health, University of California, Berkeley

Jan Morlock, East Side Neighborhood Development Corporation, St. Paul, MN

Alice O'Connor, University of Chicago, Chicago, IL

James Pickman, National Community Development Initiative, Washington, DC

Sharon Ramirez, Rainbow Research, Minneapolis, MN

Becky Saito, Search Institute, Minneapolis, MN

Harold Simon, National Housing Institute, Orange, NJ

John Smiley, Western Organization of Resource Councils, Billings, MT

JoAnn Stately, Children, Youth and Families Initiative, Bigelow Foundation, St. Paul, MN

Rebecca Stone, Chapin Hall Center For Children, University of Chicago, Chicago, IL

Patti Walter, Center for Neighborhood Technology, Chicago, IL

Marta White, The Chicago Initiative, DePaul University, Chicago, IL

Joan Winn, Chicago Community Trust, Chicago, IL

Marie Weil, School of Social Work, University of North Carolina, Chapel Hill, NC

Appendix D
Author/Factor Matrix

Across the top of this matrix are the authors whose studies we included in this review. Also across the top is the best estimate of the number of communities that were studied as part of each author's research. (In some cases, this was difficult to determine because the authors were not always

FACTORS	Almas	Arnou	Bah	Bergd	Biddl	Bruyn	Cable	Check	Clina	Cuyno	Daly	Davis	Delga	de Roux	Devel	Eisen	Ekong	Fagan	Flick
Number of communities studied	3	58	12	9	1	1	1	1	48	1	4	1	1	1	36	17	2	6	2
COMMUNITY																			
Community awareness of an issue	•					•	•	•	•	•	•	•	•	•		•	•		•
Motivation from within the community			•	•	•	•	•	•			•					•			
Small geographic area					•			•				•				•	•		
Flexibility and adaptability						•													
Preexisting social cohesion			•								•								
Ability to discuss, reach consensus, and cooperate		•					•			•		•			•				•
Existing identifiable leadership	•	•		•			•	•	•	•	•	•				•		•	
Prior success with community building							•				•								
COMMUNITY BUILDING PROCESS																			
Widespread participation	•	•		•		•	•	•	•	•		•	•	•	•	•	•	•	•
Good system of communication							•		•		•		•	•					
Minimal competition in pursuit of goals									•										
Develop self-understanding	•					•			•				•						
Benefits to many residents			•				•		•		•	•					•		
Focus on product and process concurrently									•										
Linkage to organizations outside the community							•		•			•	•		•				
Progression from simple to complex activities		•			•	•			•		•		•			•		•	•
Systematic gathering of information and analysis of community issues					•									•				•	•
Training to gain community building skills								•	•	•		•	•	•		•		•	
Early involvement and support from existing, indigenous organizations	•								•			•	•		•				
Use of technical assistance		•																	
Continual emergence of leaders, as needed				•			•					•							
Community control over decision making		•	•																•
The right mix of resources		•	•					•	•	•			•						
COMMUNITY BUILDING ORGANIZERS																			
Understanding the community	•	•							•		•					•	•		
Sincerity of commitment	•		•								•			•			•		
A relationship of trust					•	•						•	•						•
Level of organizing experience									•				•						
Able to be flexible and adaptable																			

clear about how many different communities they studied.) Down the left side of this matrix are the success factors. A "bullet" mark indicates that the author at the top of the column described that factor as having influenced the success of a community building effort.

Flora	Fried	Gave	Gitte	Glen	Hanco	Hibba	Hinsd	Hossa	Kinca	Korte	Kotlo	Leigh	Leite	Medof	Merid	Mink	Natio	Paudy	Rahm	Sibly	Sulli	Terra	Thoma	Tilak	Uphof	Vengr	Wande	Women	TOTAL
8	1	1	4	1	3	1	1	2	47	4	6	1	6	1	1	1	41	3	1	2	12	2	1	2	1	31	11	1	TOTAL
•			•	•	•		•			•		•	•	•	•	•	•		•						•			•	154
	•		•	•	•	•				•		•				•								•	•		•		119
														•															57
•					•					•	•						•							•					106
		•								•												•				•			100
				•	•	•	•	•	•	•			•	•								•	•	•					121
•	•		•	•	•		•	•		•							•	•			•	•			•			•	226
		•									•																		15
	•	•	•	•			•			•	•	•	•	•			•	•	•		•	•	•	•	•	•	•	•	323
		•	•	•		•	•			•	•	•	•	•				•	•	•	•	•						•	176
																	•												42
		•		•			•			•			•	•	•						•				•				31
										•																	•		30
		•								•			•			•					•								68
•		•		•		•	•	•	•	•				•		•	•		•		•	•		•	•		•	•	162
•		•	•				•			•				•		•		•				•	•	•	•		•	•	226
								•	•														•	•				•	24
		•	•	•		•	•	•		•			•	•		•	•		•		•			•				•	210
		•	•							•						•	•										•	•	104
•		•				•								•		•					•							•	172
•			•											•		•	•							•	•		•		69
•			•				•			•	•			•	•	•												•	133
•			•							•			•	•			•	•	•		•			•	•	•		•	245
		•																		•									138
						•			•		•						•	•											28
		•														•									•			•	13
								•							•										•				53
				•	•					•	•					•													15

Appendix E

Practical Questions for Community Builders

This is a list of the questions we developed for each community building success factor. They may be useful to assess the community work you are doing.

1. Characteristics of the Community

1A. Community Awareness of an Issue

- Are the objectives for our community building project based on the immediate concerns of the neighborhood? Can we broaden them later into a more comprehensive effort?[28]

- Do community members understand—and are they aware of—how the issues affect them?

1B. Motivation from within the Community

- Does motivation already exist in our community?

- Do people in our community have the interest to work together to address an issue?

- Do the goals and tasks in our community building effort come directly from community members?

1C. Small Geographic Area

- Is the focus for our activity within a defined and manageable geographic area?

- Do the people we are working with consider themselves part of the same community?

---

[28] Eisen (1994) makes this suggestion in her article.

1D. Flexibility and Adaptability

- Are community members open to change?

- Do community norms place rigid restrictions on the methods of a community building process? Are there ways to remove or lessen these restrictions?

- Can we switch tasks, goals, or objectives if necessary?

- Are we stuck thinking about the issues or the process of community building in one way?

1E. Preexisting Social Cohesion

- Is there a stable population of people to work with, or are people continuously moving in and out?

- Do organizations or associational groups(religious, sports, business, other) operate effectively in the community? Can they be tapped as a resource for community building efforts?

- Are there particular groups in the community that are not well connected? Are there ways to strengthen the interrelationships among these groups so all residents can participate more fully?

- Do any commonly held values among community members offer a basis for building cohesion (for example, the desire for better health services or education)?

1F. Ability to Discuss, Reach Consensus, and Cooperate

- Do the people in this community have a history of working together to solve problems or help people?

- Do any activities offer community members the opportunity to practice open dialogue, develop trust, and increase group decision-making skills?[29]

1G. Existing, Identifiable Leadership

- Does the community have members who are already taking on visible leadership positions (scout leaders, religious leaders, people who organize community events)? Are these people available and interested in doing additional community building?

- Does the community have a reservoir of leadership, as yet overlooked, in the form of leaders such as Head Start parents or block-watchers?

- What would it take to involve and train people who have not taken on leadership positions in the past?

[29] Hibbard (1986) suggested this approach in his article.

1H Prior Success with Community Building

- Does this community have a history of working with community building? Was it a successful experience?

- If it was unsuccessful, what needs to be done to increase trust and confidence in the present community building process?

- If the community has no experience, what is the best way to get started, taking some small steps, rather than moving immediately into a full-grown initiative?

2. Characteristics of the Community Building Process

2A. Widespread Participation

- Do the people participating in the community building initiative represent the population? Are some groups of community members not involved? How will this affect problem solving and decision making?

- Do mechanisms exist to help new participants feel accepted and part of the process?

- Does enough energy go into ongoing recruitment and outreach?

- What options exist to reach out to groups not already involved?

2B. Good System of Communication

- Does communication about community building activities occur in a timely way?

- Is communications a part of the overall community building process and not just an add-on responsibility?

- Does the community building effort have a variety of techniques and strategies to reach as many people as possible?

2C. Minimal Competition in Pursuit of Goals

- Do multiple community building efforts presently operate in the community? Do they all have similar activities working with the same people? Is this a source of conflict?

- Are leadership and resources in this community building effort stretched because of competition between groups?

2D. Develop Self-Understanding

- Do community members agree on important aspects of their identity? Who they represent? What geographical area they represent? What their purpose is?

- Do community members have a clear understanding of priorities?

- Does a fair process exist for making decisions?

- Do group members know what steps need to occur to accomplish tasks and ultimately to reach goals?

2E. Benefits to Many Residents

- Do goals and activities reflect the needs of most members of the community?

- Do people in the community know about the benefits expected from the community building activities and goals?

2F. Focus on Product and Process Concurrently

- Is there a balance in our community building efforts between achieving ultimate goals and paying attention to the process?

- Do we have the funding available for the process of community building that is not tied to achieving goals?[30]

2G. Linkage to Organizations Outside the Community

- Do community members have formal or informal links to people and organizations in government and other communities: If not, can they develop these links?

- Should people from outside the community be invited to join in the community building effort (for example, as members of a board or an advisory committee)?

- Do we have efforts going on to build relationships with outside agencies, political officials, the media, and funders as we are building relationships within the community?

- Have we examined other community building efforts like ours, so we can learn from them?

2H. Progression from Simple to Complex Activities

- Are the activities planned for this effort reasonable, given community members' ability to accomplish tasks?

- Does this community building effort have both long- and short-term goals as a way to develop community members' skills?[31]

---

[30] Minkler (1992) makes this suggestion in her article. Also, see O'Donnell et al., (1995).

[31] See Gittel, Vidal, and Turner (1994).

2I. Systematic Gathering of Information and Analysis of Community Issues

- Does this community building effort have enough information about the issues in the community to take action?

- Would additional information about community issues help to direct discussions? Provide background for developing solutions? Assist in solving problems and developing consensus?

2J. Training to Gain Community Building Skills

- What training do participants need in this community building effort? How can it be obtained?

- Do participants see a need for training in a particular area? What would be most beneficial?

- Is training an ongoing part of the community building process (tasks, activities, meetings are considered a learning experience), or is it a one-time effort?

- Do experienced participants train new people?

2K. Early Involvement and Support from Existing, Indigenous Organizations

- What organizations or groups in the community, such as religious congregations, parent-teacher groups, or business associations, have strong ties to the community?

- How can we recruit these groups to help with the community building effort?

2L. Use of Technical Assistance

- Could we advance our community building process faster with the help of an outside expert?

- Do we want technical assistance experts to just provide information or a service or do we want them to also be teachers?

- Will the technical experts we hire support our community building process?

2M. Continual Emergence of Leaders, as Needed

- Does this community building effort rely too heavily on the person who provided the spark for initiating the group?

- What needs does our effort have for leadership from multiple sources, and for leaders with different styles?[32]

---

[32] This is a suggestion from the *Woods Fund of Chicago, Evaluation of the Community Organizing Grant Program* (O'Donnell et al.,1995).

2N. Community Control Over Decision Making

- Do we have the flexibility in this community building effort to make decisions about how best to use funds?

- What are the needs and agendas of our funders? Do they coincide with our needs?

2O. The Right Mix of Resources

- Is the community building effort being overwhelmed by too many resources and not being allowed to build its internal strength?

- Is the community building effort at a point where it needs outside resources to grow?

- Does the community building effort include an investment of resources from within the community?

3. Characteristics of Community Building Organizers

3A. Understanding the Community

- Do the organizers for this community building effort understand how decisions are made in the community?

- Do the organizers for this community building effort understand the social norms, values, and culture of the community?

- Do the organizers of this community building effort understand the history of the community?

- Do the organizers of this community building effort understand the demographic make-up of different groups in the community and how they relate to one another?

- Do organizers of this effort understand the needs, frustrations, and problems facing the community?

3B. Sincerity of Commitment

- Do the organizers for this community building effort have the best interest of the community in mind?

- Do community members believe the organizers are fair?

- Do the organizers spend time in the community getting to know people?

- Do the organizers plan to be involved over a long period of time?

- Do the organizers stay with the effort even through the hard times to help the community overcome obstacles?

3C. A Relationship of Trust

- Has the organizer spent time developing relationships with people in the community?

- Does the person organizing this community building initiative have the skills to build trusting relationships with community members?

- Does the community organizer favor some community members over others?[33]

- Does the community organizer have the same goals and mission as the rest of the community members?

- Do community members trust the organizer will follow through on commitments?

3D. Level of Organizing Experience

- What type of experience do we want a community organizer to have?

- Do community organizer candidates for this effort have the experience needed?

- Is there training or technical assistance available to fill in the gaps in the organizer's experience?

3E Able to be Flexible and Adaptable

- Are the organizers able to adapt to changing situations, people, politics, and social climates?

- Are the organizers and the organizations they represent flexible in their approach and able to adapt to the needs of the community?

[33] Delgado (1993) makes this suggestion in his article.

Community Building Bibliography

This bibliography provides full citations for studies included in the community building research review and for research cited in the report.

1988   Almas, Reidar. "Evaluation of a Participatory Development Project in Three Norwegian Rural Communities," *Community Development Journal*, 23(1).

1992   Ameyaw, Stephen. "Sustainable Development and the Community: Lessons from the KASHA Project, Botswana," *Environmentalist*, 12(4):267-275.

1990   Arnould, Eric, J. "Changing the Terms of Rural Development: Collaborative Research in Cultural Ecology in the Sahel," *Human Organization*, 49(4):339-354.

1992   Bah, O.M. "Community Participation and Rural Water Supply Development in Sierra Leone," *Community Development Journal*, 27(1):30-41.

1993   Bergdall, Terry, D. *Methods for Active Participation—Experiences in Rural Development from East and Central Africa*. Eastern Africa: Oxford University Press.

1965   Biddle, William W. and Laureide J. Biddle. *The Community Development Process: The Rediscovery of Local Initiative*. New York: Holt, Rinehart and Winston, Inc.

1996   Blandin Foundation. *1996 Annual Report.* Grand Rapids, MN: Blandin Foundation.

1994   Bolton, Arthur. "A Strategy For Distressed Neighborhoods," in *Strategies For Distressed Neighborhood: A Report From the Center for Integrated Services For Families and Neighborhoods.* Sacramento: Western Consortium for Public Health—Center for Integrated Services.

1980   Boyte, Harry C. *The Backyard Revolution: Understanding the New Citizen Movement.* Philadelphia: Temple University Press.

1969   Brass, Reitzel, and Associates, Inc. *Community Action and Institutional Change.* Office of Economic Opportunity.

1963   Bruyn, Severyn T. *Communities in Action.* Connecticut College and University Press.

1993   Cable, Sherry. "From Fussin' to Organizing: Individual and Collective Resistance at Yellow Creek," in *Fighting Back in Appalachia: Tradition of Resistance and Change,* (Ed.) Stephen Fisher. Philadelphia: Temple University Press.

1975   Chandra, Subhash. *Urban Community Development Programme in India.* New Delhi: National Institute of Public Cooperation and Child Development.

1996   Chaskin, Robert and Prudence Brown. "Theories of Neighborhood Change," in *Core Issues in Comprehensive Community Building Initiatives.* (Ed.) Rebecca Stone. Chicago: Chapin Hall Center for Children.

1985   Checkoway, Barry. "Revitalizing an Urban Neighborhood: A St. Louis Case Study," in *The Metropolitan Midwest: Policy Problems and Prospects for Change,* (Ed.) Barry Checkoway and Carl V. Patton. Urbana, IL: University of Illinois Press.

1989   Christenson, James, A. and Jerry N. Robinson Jr. (Eds.). *Community Development in Perspective.* Ames, IA: Iowa University Press.

1970   Clinard, Marshall, B. *Slums and Community Development: Experiments in Self-Help.* New York: The Free Press.

1995   Committee for Economic Development, Research and Policy Committee, *Rebuilding Inner-City Communities: A New Approach to the Nation's Urban Crisis*. New York: Committee for Economic Development.

1989   "Cornell Empowerment Project: Empowerment through Family Support," In the *Networking Bulletin Cornell Empowerment Project* 1:2.

1976   Cottrell, L.S. Jr. "The Competent Community," Chapter in *Further Explorations in Social Psychiatry*, (Ed.) Kaplan, Wilson, and Leighton. New York: Basic Books.

1979   Cox, Fred M., John Erlich, Jack Rothman, John E. Tropman (Eds.), *Strategies of Community Organization*, Third Edition, Itasca, Illinois: F.E. Peacock Publishers, Inc.

1987   Cuyno, Rogelio. "The Soro-Soro Development Cooperative Incorporation: A Case Study on Social Development," *Regional Development Dialogue*, 8:75-97.

1978   Daley, J.M. and T. Winter. "An Evaluation of Intercultural Use of Development Methods," *Journal of the Community Development Society of America,* 9(2):62-75.

1979   Daly, John M. and Charlotte Labit. "Factors Influencing the Success of Intercultural Community Development," *Journal of the Community Development Society of America*, 10(1):67-82.

1991   Davis, John. *Contested Ground: Collective Action and the Urban Neighborhood*. Ithaca, NY: Cornell University Press.

1993   Delgado, Gary. "Building Multiracial Alliances: The Case of People United for a Better Oakland," in *Mobilizing the Community: Local Politics in the Era of the Global City*, (Eds.) Robert Fisher and J. King. Urban Affairs Annual Review, Sage.

1991   de Roux, Gustavo I. "Together Against the Computer: Par and the Struggle of Afro-Colombians for Public Services," in *Action and Knowledge: Breaking the Monopoly with Participatory Action Research*, (Ed.) O. Fals-Borda and M. Rahman. New York: Apex Press.

1976   Development Alternatives, Inc. *Strategies for Small Farmer Development: An Empirical Study of Rural Development Projects in Gambia, Ghana, Kenya, Lesotho, Nigeria, Bolivia, Columbia, Mexico, Paraguay and Peru.* Boulder: Westview Press.

1975   Effrat, Marcia Pelly. *The Community: Approaches and Applications.* New York: The Free Press.

1994   Eisen, Arlene. "Survey of Neighborhood-Based, Comprehensive Community Empowerment Initiatives," *Health Education Quarterly,* 21(2):235-252.

1982   Ekong, Ekong E., and Kamorudeen Sokoya, L. "Success and Failure in Rural Community Development Efforts: A Study of Two Cases in Southwestern Nigeria," *Community Development Journal,* 17(3): 217-224.

1994   Eng, Eugenia and Edith Parker. "Measuring Community Competence in the Mississippi Delta: The Interface Between Program Evaluation and Empowerment," *Health Education Quarterly* 21:199-220.

1987   Fagan, Jeffrey. "Neighborhood Education, Mobilization, and Organization for Juvenile Crime Prevention," *Annals of the American Academy of Political and Social Science,* 494:54-70.

1994   Flick, Louise H., Cordie Given Reese, Gail Rogers, Pamela Fletcher, and Joyce Sonn. "Building Community for Health: Lessons from a Seven-Year-Old Neighborhood/University Partnership," *Health Education Quarterly,* 21(3):369-380.

1993   Flora, Jan L., Edward Gale, Fredrick E. Schmidt, Gary P. Green, and Cornelia B. Flora. *From the Grassroots: Case Studies of Eight Rural Self-Development Efforts.* Agriculture and Rural Economy Division, Economic Research Service, U.S. Department of Agriculture. Staff Report No. AGES 9313.

1991   Freidenberg, Judith. "Participatory Research and Grassroots Development: A Case Study from Harlem," *City and Society,* 5(1):64-75.

1993   Gardner, John. *Community Building: An Overview Report and Case Profiles*. Washington D.C.: Teamworks.

1980   Gaventa, John. *Power and Powerlessness: Quiescence and Rebellion in an Appalachian Valley*. Urbana, IL: University of Illinois Press.

1994   Gittell, Ross J., Avis C. Vidal, and Robyne S. Turner. *Community Organizing as a Development Strategy: Interim Report on Palm Beach County*. New York City: Community Development Research Center, Graduate School of Management and Urban Policy, New School for Social Research.

1988   Glen, John M. *Highlander, No Ordinary School, 1932-1962*. Lexington: The University Press of Kentucky.

1979   Hancock, Samuel Lee. "Education and Rural Community Development: A Conceptual Model and Jamaican Case." Ph.D. dissertation, Virginia Polytechnic Institute and State University.

1984   Hossain, Mosharraf. "Conscientising Rural Disadvantaged Peasants Intervention through Group Action in Bangladesh: A Case Study of Proshika," in *Grassroots Participation and Self-Reliance: Experiences in South and Southeast Asia*. (Ed.) A. Rahman. Oxford Press.

1986   Hibbard, Michael. "Community Beliefs and the Failure of Community Economic Development." *Social Service Review*, 60(2):183-200.

1995   Hinsdale, Mary. *It Comes From the People: Community Development and Local Theology*. Philadelphia: Temple University Press.

1996   Joseph, Mark and Renae Ogletree. "Community Organizing and Comprehensive Community Initiatives," in *Core Issues in Comprehensive Community Building Initiatives*, (Ed.) Rebecca Stone. Chicago: Chapin Hall Center for Children.

1992   Kincaid, James M. Jr., and Edward C. Knop. *Insights and Implications From The Colorado Rural Revitalization Project, 1988-1991*. Colorado State University; University of Colorado; Colorado Department of Local Affairs; and the W.K. Kellogg Foundation.

1980   Korten, David A. "Community Organization and Rural Development: A Learning Process Approach," *Public Administration Review*, 40(5): 480-511

1995   Kotloff, Vauren J., Phoebe Roaf A., and Michelle Albert Gambone. *The Plain Talk Planning Year: Mobilizing Communities to Change*. A Report prepared for The Annie B. Casey Foundation. Philadelphia: Pubic/Private Ventures.

1995   Kubisch, Anne C., Prudence Brown, Robert Chaskin, Janice Hirota, Mark Joseph, Harold Richman, and Michelle Roberts. *Voices From the Field: Learning from Comprehensive Community Initiatives*. Draft Copy. The Roundtable on Comprehensive Community Initiatives for Children and Families. New York: The Aspen Institute

1972   Leighton, Alexander H., Edward A. Mason, Joseph C. Kern, and Frederick Leighton. "Moving Pictures as an Aid in Community Development," *Human Organization*, 31(1):11-21.

1993   Leiterman, Mindy and Joseph Stillman. *Building Community: A Report on Social Community Development Initiatives*. New York: Local Initiatives Support Corporation.

1994   Mayer, Steven E. *Building Community Capacity: The Potential of Community Foundations*. Minneapolis, Minnesota: Rainbow Research, Inc.

1986   McMillian, David W. and David M. Chavis. "Sense of Community: A Definition and Theory," *Journal of Community Psychology*, 14:6-23.

1996   McNeely, Joseph B. "Where Have All The Flowers Gone?" in *Core Issues in Comprehensive Community Building Initiatives*, (Ed.) Rebecca Stone. Chicago: Chapin Hall Center for Children.

1994   Medoff, Peter and Holly Sklar. *Streets of Hope: The Fall and Rise of an Urban Neighborhood*. Boston: South End Press.

1994   Merideth, Emily. "Critical Pedagogy and Its Application to Health Education: A Critical Appraisal of the Casa en Casa Model," *Health Education Quarterly*, 21(3):355-367

1997   Minkler, Meredith. "Community Organizing Among the Low Income Elderly in San Francisco's Tenderloin District," in *Community Organizing and Community Building for Health*, (Ed.) Meredith Minkler. New Brunswick, N.J.: Rutgers University Press, In Press.

1992   Minkler, Meredith. "Community Organizing Among the Elderly Poor in the United States: A Case Study," *International Journal of Health Services,* 22(2): 303-316

1985   Minkler, Meredith. "Building Supportive Ties and Sense of Community among the Inner-City Elderly: The Tenderloin Senior Outreach Project," *Health Education Quarterly,* 12(4):303-314

1979   The National Commission on Neighborhoods. *People, Building Neighborhoods: Case Study* Appendix Vol. I, *Final Report to The President and The Congress of The United States*. Superintendent of Documents. Washington, D.C.: U.S. Government Printing Office.

1979   The National Commission on Neighborhoods. *People Building Neighborhoods: Case Study* Appendix Vol. II, *Final Report to the President and The Congress of the United States*. Superintendent of Documents, U.S. Government Printing Offices. Washington, D.C.

1975   National Research Council, *Toward an Understanding of Metropolitan American*. San Francisco: Canfield Press.

1995   O'Donnell, Sandra, Yvonne Jeffries, Frank Sanchez, and Pat Selmi. *Woods Fund of Chicago Evaluation of the Funds Community Organizing Grant Program, Executive Summary and Findings and Recommendations of the Evaluation Team*. Chicago: Woods Funds of Chicago.

1997   Patton, Michael Quinn. *Utilization-Focused Evaluation*, third edition. Thousand Oaks, California: Sage Publications.

1992   Paudyal, Durga Prasad. "Deedar: A Success Story in Cooperative Village Development," *Community Development Journal,* 27(3): 274-284.

1984   Rahman, A. "The Small Farmer Development Programme of Nepal," in *Grassroots Participation and Self-Reliance: Experiences in South and Southeast Asia*. (Ed.) A. Rahman. Oxford Press.

1992   Rivera, Felix and John Erlich. *Community Organizing in a Diverse Society*. Needham Heights, MA: Allyn and Bacon Press

1986   Rubin, Herbert J. and Irene Rubin. *Community Organizing and Development*. Columbus, Ohio: Merrill Publishing Company.

1969   Sibley, Willis E. "Social Organization, Economy, and Directed Cultural Change in Two Philippine Barrios," *Human Organization*, 28(2): 148-154.

1993   Sullivan, Mercer L. *More Than Housing: How Community Development Corporations Go About Changing Lives and Neighborhoods*. New York City: Community Development Research Center Graduate School of Management and Urban Policy, New School for Social Research.

1996   Stone, Rebecca. "Introduction," in *Core Issues in Comprehensive Community-Building Initiatives*, (Ed.) Rebecca Stone. Chicago: Chapin Hall.

1986   Terrant, James and Hasan Poerbo. "Strengthening Community-Based Technology Management Systems," in *Community Management Asian Experience and Perspectives,* (Ed.) David C. Korten. Connecticut: Kumarian Press.

1989   Thomas-Slayter, Barbara P. and Richard Ford. "Water, Soils, Food, and Rural Development: Examining Institutional Frameworks in Katheka Sublocation," *Canadian Journal of African Studies*, 23(2):250-271.

1984   Tilakaratna, S. "Grassroots Self-Reliance in Sri Lanka: Organizations of Betel and Coir Yarn Producers," in *Grassroots Participation and Self-Reliance: Experiences in South and Southeast Asia*. (Ed.) A. Rahman. Oxford Press.

1986   Uphoff, Norman. "Activating Community Capacity for Water Management in Sri Lanka," in *Community Management Asian Experience and Perspectives,* (Ed.) David C. Korten. Connecticut: Kumarian Press.

1974   Vengroff, Richard. "Popular Participation and the Administration of Rural Development: The Case of Botswana," *Human Organization*, 33(3):303-309.

1985   Wandersman, Abraham, Richard Roth and John Prestby. "Keeping Community Organizations Alive," *Citizen Participation,* 6(4):16-19.

1987   Wanyande, Peter. "Women's Groups in Participatory Development: Kenya's Development Experience through the Use of Harambee," *Development: Seeds of Change,* 2(3):95-102.

1963   Warren, Roland L. *The Community in America.* Chicago: Rand McNally Press.

1984   Women's Research Committee, Farmers' Assistance Board, Inc., and Women's Health Movement. "The Struggle toward Self-Reliance of Organized Resettled Women in the Philippines," in *Grassroots Participation and Self-Reliance: Experiences in South and Southeast Asia.* (Ed.) A. Rahman. Oxford Press.

NOTES

NOTES

NOTES

Collaboration Handbook: Creating, Sustaining, and Enjoying the Journey

by Michael Winer and Karen Ray

Everything you need for a successful collaboration. Shows you how to get a collaboration going, define the results you're after, determine everyone's roles, create an action plan, and evaluate the results. This valuable guide tells you what to expect and how to handle challenges in a way that strengthens your group. Includes a case study of one collaboration from start to finish, helpful tips on how to avoid pitfalls, and worksheets to keep everyone on track.

192 pages, softcover, $28.00

Collaboration: What Makes It Work

by Wilder Research Center

Use this report to see if your collaboration's plans include the necessary ingredients! This report gives you an in-depth review of current collaboration research in the health, social science, education, and public affairs fields. Major findings are summarized, critical conclusions drawn, and nineteen key factors influencing successful collaborations are identified.

53 pages, softcover, $14.00

Marketing Workbook for Nonprofit Organizations Volume I: Develop the Marketing Plan

by Gary J. Stern

Don't just wish for results—get them! This book shows you how to create a straightforward, usable marketing plan. It includes the 6 P's of Marketing—and how to use them effectively—a sample marketing plan, and detachable worksheets.

132 pages, softcover, $25.00

Marketing Workbook for Nonprofit Organizations Volume II: Mobilize People for Marketing Success

by Gary J. Stern

Put together a successful promotional campaign based on the most persuasive tool of all: personal contact! This book shows you how to mobilize your entire organization, its staff, volunteers, and supporters in a focused, one-to-one marketing campaign. Provides step-by-step instruction, sample agendas for motivational trainings, and worksheets to keep the campaign organized and on track.

Also includes *My Personal Marketing Plan,* a pocket guide available for all your representatives. In it, they can record key campaign messages and find motivational reminders.

192 pages, softcover, $25.00

Strategic Planning Workbook for Nonprofit Organizations, Revised and Updated

by Bryan Barry

Chart a wise course for your nonprofit's future. This workbook gives you practical step-by-step guidance, real-life examples, one nonprofit's complete strategic plan, and easy-to-use worksheets.

144 pages, softcover, $25.00

The Little Book of Peace

Illustrated by Kelly O. Finnerty

A pocket-size guide to help people think about violence, and talk about it with their families and friends. We hope this booklet will be a tiny start toward making the world a more peaceful place.

24 pages, .65 each (minimum order 10 copies)

What Works in Preventing Rural Violence

by Wilder Research Center

An in-depth review of 88 effective strategies to respond to rural violence. Also includes a Community Report Card with step-by-step directions on how you can collect, record, and use information about violence in your community.

94 pages, softcover, $17.00

Foundations for Violence-Free Living

A Step-by-Step Guide to Facilitating Men's Domestic Abuse Groups

by David J. Mathews, MA, LICSW

A complete guide to facilitating a men's domestic program. Includes 29 activities, detailed guidelines for presenting each activity, and a discussion of psychological issues that may arise out of each activity. Also gives you tips for intake, individual counseling, facilitating groups, working with resistant clients, and recommended policies and releases.

240 pages, softcover, $45.00

On the Level

(Participant's Workbook to Foundations for Violence-Free Living)

Men can record their insights and progress as they build a new foundation for violence-free living. Contains 49 worksheets including midterm and final evaluations. A permanent binding makes the workbook easy to carry home for outside assignments and you don't have to make any trips to the copy machine.

160 pages, softcover, $15.00

Four easy ways to order

 Call toll-free: **1-800-274-6024**
8:00 am to 4:00 pm CST
(in Mpls./St. Paul: 612-659-6024)

Fax order form to: **612-642-2061** (24 hours a day)

Mail order form to: A. H. Wilder Foundation
Publishing Center
919 Lafond Avenue
St. Paul, MN 555104

E-mail your order to: **books@wilder.org**

Shipping

Standard Charges: *If order totals:*   *Add:*

Up to $30.00	$4.00
$30.01 - 60.00	$5.00
$60.01 - 150.00	$6.00
$150.01 - 500.00	$8.00
Over $500.00	3% of order

- Orders are shipped UPS or Parcel Post. Please allow two weeks for delivery.
- For orders outside the U.S. or Canada, please add an additional U.S. $5.00
- Special RUSH delivery is available. Please call our toll-free phone number for rates.

NO-RISK GUARANTEE

We believe in our publications and want you to use them. When your order arrives, examine it carefully. If you are not satisfied for any reason, simply return it within 30 days for a replacement, credit, or refund.

Save money when you order in quantity

We offer substantial discounts on orders of ten or more copies of any single title. Please call for more information.

Send us your manuscript

Wilder Publishing Center continually seeks manuscripts and proposals for publications in the fields of nonprofit management and development, community development, and violence prevention. Send us your proposal or manuscript. Or, if you'd like more information, call us toll-free at 1-800-274-6024 and ask for our Author Guidelines.

Order Form

	QTY.	PRICE EACH	TOTAL AMOUNT
Collaboration Handbook: Creating, Sustaining, and Enjoying the Journey		$28.00	
Collaboration: What Makes It Work		14.00	
Community Building: What Makes It Work		20.00	
Foundations for Violence-Free Living		45.00	
On the Level (participant's workbook to Foundation's for Violence-Free Living)		15.00	
The Little Book of Peace (minimum order 10 copies)		0.65	
Marketing Workbook for Nonprofit Organizations Volume I: Develop the Marketing Plan		25.00	
Marketing Workbook for Nonprofit Organizations Volume II: Mobilize People for Marketing Success		25.00	
Strategic Planning Workbook for Nonprofit Organizations, Revised and Updated		25.00	
What Works in Preventing Rural Violence		17.00	
		SUBTOTAL	
In MN, please add 7% sales tax or attach exempt certificate			
		SHIPPING	
		TOTAL	

Amherst H. Wilder Foundation
Publishing Center
919 Lafond Avenue
St. Paul, MN 55104

Toll-Free 1-800-274-6024
Fax: (612) 642-2061

Name _____

Title _____

Organization _____

Address _____

_____

City _____ State _____ Zip _____

Phone *(in case we have questions)* (_____) _____

Payment Method: VISA   MasterCard   AMERICAN EXPRESS **Cards**

Card # _____

Expiration Date _____

Signature (required) _____

☐ Check/Money Order (payable to A.H. Wilder Foundation)

☐ Bill Me   Purchase Order No. _____